Ellen,
Thanks for your great community work.
Best
Joe

In the Streets ... In the Suites

In the Streets ... In the Suites

A former Catholic priest's remarkable work in connecting the rich and the poor to deal with life's basic challenges

Joe Selvaggio
and
Jim Stowell

ISBN 0-9615951-3-2

Cover Design by Jim Lotter

Printed in the United States of America by Bolger Concept to Print.

In Memory of
James P. Shannon
A much-admired teacher, mentor, and friend.

Contents

Acknowledgments

My editor, Doug Benson, sent me an e-mail saying I was "one lucky guy" to have so many talented friends who were willing to send me content suggestions and encourage me as I tried to survive the struggle to write and publish a book. He is certainly correct!

So, eternal gratitude goes to Doug and others.

For content suggestions: Tony Bouza, Jen Larson, Cathy Madison, Tony Morely, Tuny and Michael O'Rourke, Lisa Perez, Neal St. Anthony, Mike Stephen, Becky Stewart, Terry Thompson and Billie Young.

For actual pieces describing our work together: Tony Bouza, Burt Cohen, Susan Flagler, Ed Flahavan, John Hartwell, Frank Kroncke, Dick McFarland, Ted Pouliot, Steve Rothschild, James P. Shannon, Terry Thompson, Dan Turner, and George Wertin.

Playwright Jim Stowell deserves special thanks, along with the Great American History Theatre and of course my recipient son, Sam, my patient wife, Rose, and my "providers," PPL & staff.

Thank you, thank you, thank you! These thanks (and maybe an eternal reward in the next life) take the place of monetary payments.

—**Joe Selvaggio**

Editor's Note

by Doug Benson

As Tony Bouza notes in the foreword to this book, the attempt to understand another human being is a formidable undertaking. The attempt to totally understand what makes another person tick is invariably doomed to failure.

Nevertheless, some people live so far outside the norm, and do it so successfully, and seem so contented, that we can't help but want to know how they came to be who they are.

Joe Selvaggio is such a person. And he's complicated. In fact, The Great American History Theatre decided Joe's life and personality are so interesting, so multifaceted, that it commissioned a play about him, titled *Joe.* In it, the playwright, Jim Stowell, says, "There are many Joes. People who work with or know Joe talk of the many Joes. There is Saint Joe. Demon Fund-Raiser Joe. Bad-Taste-Joke Joe. Bad-Tie Funny-Dressing Joe. Organized Joe. Forgetful Joe. When he was young he was Drift-Along Joe. He was Priest Joe and then Rebel Priest Joe. Protester Joe. Organizer Joe. Husband and Father Joe. Maddening Joe. Whiner Joe. Relentless Joe. But let us never forget Generous Joe—Joe the little guy with a very big heart."

The "Joe Play," as it has come to be known, inspired us to produce a "Joe Book." (I say "us" because I had already been working with Joe on another book tentatively entitled "Letters to Sam," which has been put on temporary hiatus.) Rather than producing a biography or an autobiography, however, which would suffer from the limitations imposed by a single point of view—that of the biographer or of the autobiographer—we've tried to tap into the insights of several people who've come to know Joe over the years: close friends, seminary classmates, people he's helped to achieve their life goals, the playwright Jim Stowell, and others. Each has a unique perspective on this remarkable guy, Joe Selvaggio. We've also included Joe's own reflections on how he came to be who he is, do what he does, and think the way he thinks about each of a dozen subject areas, followed by Joe's own recounting of the "arc" of his life.

Each chapter starts with an excerpt from the play *Joe,* or the observations of one or more of the many people whose lives Joe has touched, or both. These comments are followed by Joe's own thoughts on the subject, in the form of a letter to his adult son Sam.

Doug Benson is a freelance writer and editor who lives in Minneapolis. He thought meeting Joe Selvaggio through a friend was just a happy accident until he discovered that almost everyone he knows is a friend of Joe.

Foreword

Introducing Joe Selvaggio

by Tony Bouza

It is hard to imagine a greater act of presumption than to undertake anyone's biography. The attempt involves entering another's skin, brain and heart, thereby enabling our complete mastery of that person's nature. The exertion seems counter to our knowledge of our own dark predilections and unfathomable fears, ambitions, secret desires, and hopes. We know, instinctively, how difficult we are to be fully understood and quail at the thought of anyone's actually reading our minds. Voltaire said, "I've never heard of a crime of which I didn't feel myself capable." This goes to the heart of the matter and, as Joseph Conrad understood, that is a dark place indeed.

Yet our hubris is such as to drive us to blithely and confidently attempt it anyway. The effort, though, ought to be tempered with the humility that recognizes the limits of understanding and warns the reader. Be warned.

I dubbed Joe Selvaggio "Urban Saint" when a reporter from *Minnesota Monthly* Magazine called to ask me about him. The phrase was apt and carefully distilled over the years I've known Joe and became a sobriquet as it adorned the cover of the magazine. I had long before, in an extended public life, learned the importance of labels, latterly described as "sound bites." In fact, there are few more valuable lessons to be learned than to develop a taste for converting thorny issues into punchy one-liners.

I first met Joe almost a quarter century earlier, when I arrived in Minneapolis to be the police department chief. I'd been out of work for five months, having been summarily fired as No. 2 of the New York City Transit Police, by an unhappy mayor, in Sept. 1979. I'd been in St. Paul once, years earlier, to speak to women cops and had been astounded to learn that the river lazily easing below my window was the mighty Mississippi. So I knew virtually no one and I needed to learn the players.

Who were for real? And who were the fakes and charlatans? A police chief is as political a figure as the mayor or any council member. Evaluation of our *dramatis personae* can't be left to chance.

In the halls of power—whether political, corporate or philanthropic—the currency of choice is solid information. I walked about to examine projects and operations. How many kids attended Boys Club facilities? Did this person follow through and deliver or was it bullshit? Were those professing to do so really feeding the hungry, housing the homeless, clothing the naked? It was not hard to identify the poverty pimps and operators—and there were a lot more of them than of the genuine doers.

I'd wander in on coffee klatches, discover staffers flying first class and occupying fancy offices or kiting administrative expenses. Entire industries seemed to be devoted to separating foundations from their funds with great stories that proved mere fairy tales. I rapidly calculated the few winners and many losers and marveled, again, at the difficulty of achieving the noblest intentions of altruism because of the cunning of the petitioners. And few, with the notable exception of the now deceased Russell Ewald of the McKnight Foundation, bothered to traipse to the field to see just how the dollars were being spent. Management By Walking About (MBWA) was then, and is now, an unpracticed art.

Foundations calcified in bureaucratic mazes while petitioners frittered millions away. The more I saw of them, the keener my appreciation of friends who advocated dispensing with the foundations' endowments altogether.

When I got to Sharing and Caring Hands, however, I saw hundreds of bedraggled souls lined up for food. Mary Jo Copeland fed, clothed and housed society's flotsam, and even knelt to wash their feet. I loved what she did, but her religious fervor prevented me from getting close. I'd champion her cause, help in any way I could, but we'd never be personal friends. She was storing up credits in heaven and performing miracles of salvation.

I saw no such missionary fervor in Joe Selvaggio, who was then, in 1980, in the eighth year of running Project for Pride in Living (PPL). His tenure would extend to a quarter of a century at its helm. PPL ran housing, employment and similar help programs, but these are abstract phrases that melt before the reality of actual human need. The numbers are mere statistics; the faces convey tragedy.

Joe had served as a Catholic priest, but left the priesthood as his sense of service gradually overcame the love of ritual, magic, and mystery of a Church that treasured obedience and that seemed to take Jesus' actual ministry as either irrelevant or downright subversive. It's hard to imagine Joe's consenting to the title "Father." Libido was also a factor in his return to the laity. It always tickled me to read how Mahatma Gandhi slept with young women so he might resist the all-too-human urges to which the rest of us would unfailingly give in. Joe struck me as being more in our camp, on this one, than Gandhi's. In other ways, though, he did remind me of the Indian saint.

Joe is strange. Mumbly, boyish, giggly while seemingly unfocused, he appears to stumble ineffectually through life. His is the most unprepossessing style imaginable. There is nothing remotely finished or polished about the man. He dresses as he must, but can rarely resist a ribald tie. He mails postcards of such salacious nature as to risk a beheading in Riyadh. Like a character from Voltaire, he is a naïf, but an inspired one.

When I met Joe he was married to Phoebe, living in a large, oldish house in a mostly black neighborhood. Joe and Phoebe were both working, both active in the community, with a son, Sam, in Phoebe's womb, when they learned of two boys,

Ricardo and Anthony, who needed a family. They said, "Why not us?" and within four months they had three sons. I didn't know him that well then, so I can't speak to the factors that drove him and Phoebe apart, but I do know they're still friends. Their parting might have involved the mischievous, childish, innocent phase of his nature. Joe never struck any of us—his closest friends—as one who would be especially easy to be married to. There were too many other claims on his energies.

I'd run into Joe here and there as I involved myself in programs that helped the poor. To me, this was crime prevention at its most effective. I had the nutty notion that the overclass was busily manufacturing criminals through neglect, racism and economic oppression. I got into real trouble when I wrote that the most cost-effective crime prevention measure undertaken in the last half of the 20th century was 1973's Roe vs. Wade decision that enabled about a quarter of a million impoverished teenagers to have abortions annually. This sharply reduced the "at risk" male populations that produced so much street crime.

And since street crime was my number-one concern, I was keenly aware of anything that might mitigate its impact. Hence my deep interest in programs involved in working with the underclass—Joe's territory.

In the course of time, I learned that a young woman, Rosario Escañan, needed to flee the Philippines to escape the wrath of President Ferdinand Marcos—a dictator who brooked no opposition. She needed someone to marry her to bring her to America. Joe offered himself and, as his is wont—to beg for causes he believes in—asked for money for fare. Erica and I gave him $100. Rose had been battling the dictatorship long before it became fashionable.

Rose and Joe married and moved into the big house. In the fullness of time I got a check for $100 with a note stating that they'd fallen in love and felt that keeping our contribution was somehow wrong. That's Joe.

Rose is a tiny, lovely, child-like woman who seemed to be the perfect foil as we dubbed Joe a pedophile for taking up with this little girl. She was then, of course, in her mid-thirties.

And that's Joe, too.

He is a hopeless amalgam of venial sins and enormous virtues. It is his sins that make him human. The breadth of his spirit includes taking a poor black female neighbor to the hoity toity Minneapolis Club for lunch without a blink. He includes the excluded in his life and they spill into all his activities. That would certainly be a prime source of tension with anyone sharing his life.

Once I had to do a set of profiles of people whose lives had been touched by PPL. An Asian gentleman came to see me, fresh from cleaning toilets in a hospital. He was around fifty. How had PPL changed his life? "Mister Joe," he said, "I met him in Vietnam. I'd been a colonel in the South Vietnamese Army and had been sent to a work camp by the communists. I lifted logs all day. Mister Joe said he'd try to help me and sponsored my coming to America with my family. Mister Joe got me this job." The way he said "Mister Joe" made me wish for a similar eulogy on my demise.

Joe's receptionist carried a baby and had a child on her back as she crossed the Rio Grande in chest-high, swirling waters at night.

Joe helped a Chinese family from Vietnam open a restaurant that led to the opening of a vast new eatery, other large enterprises, a determined march through the "U" (the universal appellation, in Minnesota, for the state university) and confident entrance—by the whole family—into the upper middle-class in the space of about 15 years.

The thing that struck me about all the folks that I encountered was the direct, personal involvement of Mister Joe in all their lives. PPL was a vehicle he created that enabled him to help folks to lift themselves in the classic style of bootstrappism.

Joe spends his life in the trenches. His is a hugely personal commitment. He built a shopping mall at Chicago and Franklin—the epicenter of the city's decay—and then secured tenants, many of whom were folks he'd helped in other ways. Then he pressed the cops to pester the drug dealers and spent countless hours with the shop owners, offering counsel, helping them survive and providing moral support. He attends Council meetings, lobbies mayors and jounces bureaucrats. Total immersion.

What all this personal engagement—mostly done rather unconsciously and automatically—gets him is the most valuable asset available—credibility. In an age of jukers, jivers, slippers, sliders and slicksters, Joe is the goods, an almost Biblical figure ministering to the people from the bully pulpit of the street.

And all of this adds up to a sort of capital that can only be gained through good work. Joe is a demon fund-raiser.

I always thought nothing could be easier than to give money to help good causes. What could be more intuitive? Or, as it turns out, more wrong. It is tough to translate bucks into real help.

Rich folks in Minnesota often come with a Midwestern Protestant form of populism that drives them to good work. Many discover their efforts exploited and are chastened in the hubris that opening the checkbook eliminates many ills. So they turn to the folks who deliver real results—the Mary Jo Copelands and Joe Selvaggios and, amazingly, there aren't very many of them. In fact, for me, they stand, uniquely, as a pretty lonely pair.

Equally amazingly, both Joe and Mary Jo learned the importance of accessing this source of wealth, worked hard to cultivate contacts among the rich and developed vehicles to facilitate the giving. Mary Jo will say, "We're going to raise $8 million and house a hundred families," with such ebullient assurance as to include no possibility of failure. Watching Joe work a room of the state's movers is to watch a fumbling, mumbling master of meandering understatement generate treasures for his causes.

Joe is wonderfully coachable because, like Socrates, he is always searching and questioning. The doctrinaire, the sleek, the positive and the professional are alien to his nature and approach. And he listens hard.

When I first heard him speak, I thought, "Demosthenes, only with the rocks still in." Gradually I came to appreciate that his halting, understated style was the very wellspring of his genuineness, and I decided the stones should stay.

And he's brave, too. In addition to stopping speeding bullets, runaway trains and scaling tall buildings, Joe has that humble, unostentatious courage that deflects credit with a charming, vulnerable humility.

Ask him about his grotesquely bent pinkie and he'll laugh and describe how a bully threw him down on the sidewalk when he protested at a church. Another time, he'll describe how he tentatively foot-felt his way out to a drowning boy, longingly gazing at the safety of the beach and wishing fervently for help when a benign wave moved the boy's body to Joe's grasp. Then he'll reluctantly describe a scene of comic ineptitude as the boy vomits water and basically comes to life, unaided by the fitful ministrations of well-meaning helpers.

And Joe doesn't lack for moral courage, either, although you'd have to pry from him the admission that he's been arrested for peace demonstrating, civil disobedience, or protesting some wrong against the poor. Joe is the kind of guy who doesn't accept oppression quietly and isn't content to watch even an unliked neighbor dragged off.

And he is not mean-spirited, jealous, or even competitive. He will speak generously of rivals and give a thoughtful, fair assessment of anyone or any issue, yet couch it in kind language. Despite the sweetness, however, this candor has, predictably, landed him in hot water, especially with bishops, CEOs and pompous politicians.

Joe's approach is rooted in the knowledge that no one can really help anyone. All we can do is help others help themselves. Accountability, individual responsibility, consequence and all those hard teachings that life will deliver are woven into housing, employment and educational programs. The motto is old, trite, overdone, yet still true: "Give people a fish and they will eat for a day—teach them to fish and they will eat for a lifetime."

Joe is funny. He carries an amazing little book that not only contains a busy calendar but the names and phone numbers of important folks. It also contains listings of dirty jokes he takes a little boy's giggly delight in repeating. He rarely gets to the punch line before breaking up.

Joe's inquisitive nature makes him great company. I can go around Lake Calhoun and keep a bristling discussion going with him on scores of topics. His is a speculative mind focused on such questions as poverty and wealth, racism, social justice or the influence of religion.

Joe never earned over $50,000 as CEO of PPL, an enterprise with a multimillion dollar annual budget, and he left without a pension, hoping social security and a small savings fund would provide. PPL's offices were modest houses in poor neighborhoods, much like the one he's always occupied nearby. He will make a sincere attempt at discussing money issues and even profess a wholesome appreciation of its utility, but he doesn't mean it.

Joe remains connected to PPL by helping with its capital campaign and such, but he has spent most of his time lately working on the One Percent Club he founded. Its purpose is to get wealthy folks to contribute one percent or more of their net worth annually to charity. He will even help select a beneficiary if asked. In a highly charitable state, hundreds of Minnesota's rich have signed up (an average of 10 per month since the programs' beginning in 1997). This has accelerated the giving dramatically.

In a surprisingly rare recognition of his value, the Northwest Area and Grotto Foundations awarded him the first Louis W. Hill, Jr. Fellowship in 2003 for his altruism. It carries some academic, lecturing and writing responsibilities as well as a stipend of $100,000. The award was almost magnetically drawn to the most deserving champion of the shirtless in the state.

We've vacationed with Joe and Rose many times and have had them as guests, and it is clear that neither is driven by the slightest consideration of financial security. Both are great company and fun to be with, but it is impossible to avoid the suspicion that Joe needs looking after.

Joe can be tough, but usually only in defense of a principle or a project. Tenacious as a mussel, he will not give in on a question centering on human plight. The underclass never had a more quixotic, yet effective, fighter.

Tending to think of such a paragon as St. Francis of Assisi as little more than an ambulatory bird feeder, I'm mostly skeptical of saints. To be believable to me, they must be engaged in altruism yet be flawed enough to be comfortably human.

Listening to Joe describe how his nonagenarian mother was slipping through his arms towards the frozen tundra of a Minnesota sidewalk in January, because of his "inadequate upper arm strength," is to hear a man not hung up on questions of self-image. In this account, Joe's lack of ego shines as he makes fun of his weakness. The hero, as it turns out, is a black neighbor who rescues his slumping mother before her total descent to the frozen surface.

He'd taken his mother into his home after his brother died and looked after her until she had to be put in a care facility. There he lunched with her every day until she died. Just after her 100th birthday.

Joe's been arrested and has been beaten up and has wound up on his ass in postures any of us would find humiliating, yet such is his own modesty and humility that he describes the events with not a trace of embarrassment.

Marriage to (and friendship with) Joe means sharing life with the countless hordes Joe has helped. His interest never flags. He once reproved me for walking away from someone he'd introduced me to. "You were bored," he said, "and opted to wander off." He was right. Not only would he have stayed, but it would never have occurred to him to be bored.

Greatness comes from engagement in life's timeless questions. What is its meaning? What is our obligation? Who am I? What shall I do with my life?

I've known Joe now for almost a quarter century, as a really close friend. It is only this that gives me the courage to attempt to convey an impression of the man. He is an urban saint, but in the spirit of Graham Greene's saint in "The Power and the Glory," he is fully, thunderously human and delightfully flawed. It is the flaws that ultimately convince me of his greatness, because their existence persuade me that some hideous truth is not being concealed. The recesses of the human spirit can easily hide enormous—even frightening—possibilities, but I think and hope I know Joe well enough to convey a reasonably accurate view of the full man at 66.

Joe Selvaggio asks key questions. Joe Selvaggio lives his answers.

Tony Bouza was born in Spain and moved to the U.S. at age nine. He was a New York City cop until his 50s, when he became Chief of Police in Minneapolis, Minnesota. He is retired.

1. Safety and Neighborhoods

From the play *Joe,* by Jim Stowell

See a woman's face as she opens the door to her first home. She has dark skin. She came here as an illegal alien. Through twists and turns she ended up in Minneapolis in the Phillips neighborhood. She had several children and one day the husband/father just disappeared out of their lives. That did not destroy her or her family. By word of mouth she heard about the job training program at Project for Pride in Living (PPL). She took the course. She got a job. Months later she got a car. And now, with the help of PPL, she was opening the door on the first home she had ever owned in her life.

See her face. You will see a joy there so intense that it makes her cry. This feeling about our own home is something that is a part of all of us. Something that is connected inside the very core of our species—connected back to the first fire; back to the first cave. See her face now as she looks on her home and you are seeing that cave connection being made and that primeval dream come true.

See her face now and you will see pride. Pride in where she has come from to where she stands at this moment. It is not the kind of pride that goes before the fall, but the kind of pride that she has earned and has a right to feel, standing where she is standing at this moment, in the doorway of her home. See her face now and you will know what dignity looks like.

Now hear the voices of her children as they run up the front walk and into the empty rooms of the house, soon to be filled with their own belongings. Hear the voices of the children as they run from room to room. See the face of a little boy and little girl as they open the doors on their rooms! No longer sleeping four to a bed... now they will have their own beds and even their own rooms! See the joy on those children's faces! You are seeing pride and dignity there as well.

Now see the woman's face again as she watches her children run into the house and fill up the rooms with life. You will see a slightly different kind of joy there, but still a joy so intense that it makes her want to cry again. You will see another slightly different kind of pride there as she watches her children play in her home—their home. You see her face watching her children's joy and you see a deepened dignity there.

Creating this kind of scene is why Joe Selvaggio started PPL. There are many Joes. ... But let us never forget Generous Joe—Joe, the little guy with a very big heart.That's not sentimental hogwash either. A house that becomes a home is more than just a building. When that lady opened the door to that house, she was opening the door to her dream. That's what a home is: a dream coming true.

That lady looked right at me and pointed at Joe and said, "That man is my hero." Considering all she has struggled through in her life, such a compliment must be taken seriously. At the time, I was stunned. Joe looked a little stunned himself. I had never been in a room where someone referred to another person in the room as their hero. Hero Joe. He is Hero Joe because he is all those other Joes. And especially because of Generous, Big-Hearted Joe. He is still doing what he set out to do when he became a priest: trying to make the earth as heavenly as possible.

From Joe's letters to Sam

Dear Sam,

When our little group of do-gooders from St. Joan of Arc Church offered to sell Alice McHie her first home she said to me, "I'm not going to live in no ghetto, you know."

I was a bit surprised to hear Alice say that because Alice was a pretty grass-roots black woman who had never lived in a middle class neighborhood in her entire life. There is the instinct to suspect uppityness when someone is just, and justly, asserting their right to a view of their own. But when I talked to her about it I found out what she was really saying was "I need a decent, safe neighborhood to raise my kids in. I don't need crime and temptation for my kids all around."

I assured Alice that the house we had picked out for her as affordable was in a "mixed neighborhood"—that there were basically all single family homes and no higher crime rates than other neighborhoods. When she saw the house and walked the block, she was satisfied.

Since I had never lived in a high crime area I didn't fully appreciate Alice's concern. It wasn't long, however, before your mother and I were looking for a home and we had to ask ourselves the same question. Is this neighborhood one where we'll feel safe from burglars and our kids can play in the streets?

The time had come for us to sink our roots into a neighborhood and build a family. I know I didn't want to live in the suburbs, or even in a middle class neighborhood in the city. I was a big Kennedy family fan, and I didn't want people to say about me what they said about the Kennedys, namely, "Sure the Kennedys can push for integration because they can afford to live in a place like Hyannis Port and not feel the consequences of integrated neighborhoods." I needed to live with both blacks and the poor to remain true to my convictions.

I remember when we were looking at buying 3320 5th Ave. S. I saw Oliver Medlock across the street and went over and introduced myself. I quickly learned that Oliver was about 10 years older than I, and had a wife and 10 kids. He told me he was the pastor of a small Baptist Church over on 4th Ave. I told him of my clergy background so he wouldn't take offense at the big question I wanted to ask him.

"Oliver," I said, as the soul music blasted from a neighbor's window, "are white folks accepted well in this neighborhood?"

"Oh sure." He replied, "They'll steal from you just as soon as they'll steal from me. No prejudice."

While I wasn't totally reassured by his answer, I felt the man had a sense of humor, and was telling me that I'd be treated like anyone else. I knew he'd be a good neighbor, so we decided to buy the house.

Over the years the neighborhood has been okay. One summer it was pretty bad. We had 3 drug houses on the block, and two murders within 12 months. Then we got a little help from a neighborhood group called Summit Academy O.I.C. (Occupational Industrialization Center).

Louis King, the executive director of Summit came over with about 12 teenagers on Saturday morning and started sweeping the street. Neighbors came out to help and we were having a good time. After the cleanup, Louis started the grill with some hot charcoal and the speeches began. Different neighbors were asked to come up and use the bullhorn to address the small crowd. When it came to Serita Medlock's turn (Serita is Oliver's daughter who bought the house just North of us) she announced to the crowd that she was going to say her piece to some bad elements on the block. She walked across the street and started yelling through the bullhorn into a bedroom window, "No more drugs! No more drugs! This is our neighborhood. We won't take it anymore. We're staying. You must go. No more Drugs! No more Drugs!"

"That gal is brave," I thought. Those nuts in that house have guns. But that's what it takes to get rid of those drug houses. They actually moved at the end of the month. Improving the neighborhood is, as it was in Stalingrad, a house-to-house battle.

By and large, it's been a livable neighborhood. I don't know if the Medlocks would agree. Their family did experience one really big tragedy that they'll have to live with forever. It involved Serita's nephew, Bobby. Bobby was about 16. He used to cut our grass on occasion—a decent kid, but he started hanging around the wrong guys. Apparently he got recruited into one of the gangs. One night when the gang members were gathered at one of the houses, Bobby started mouthing off. One "tougher than thou" gang member lost his temper and shot Bobby twice, in the head. Bobby ended up in the hospital and then in rehab for months. It devastated the family and divided their energy. Some of their "spirit" is gone, but they are still great neighbors.

Bobby still walks around the neighborhood with a severe limp. He barely speaks anymore—doesn't go to school—just hangs out. I'd like to get Charlton Heston to help take care of Bobby the way the Medlocks have had to. Heston would probably sneer at the suggestion that he and his NRA are keeping our neighborhood unsafe.

To me it follows like smoke from fire.

Love,

Dad

P.S. When you're looking for your first house, I'd wager that *safety* will be your first concern.

2. The Need for Others' Approval

From the Play *Joe*

"Our parents wanted us to study but didn't really teach us a lot," Joe said. "They sort of felt a little bit inferior in that they only had a fourth grade and an eighth grade education. [My older brother] John and I were becoming real Americans, while their roots were still back in the old country. So they just let us be happy with our friends and our games. They just weren't too intrusive into our lives. I think it worked fine." It was a growing-up very unlike that of a friend of his, Karen Hanson, a woman who was brought up by a father and mother who were Communists. The father was a labor organizer and both parents were political activists their entire lives. Karen's father was even arrested for passing out leaflets in support of the Social Security Act before it was passed.

Joe's friend Karen had been a part of that for her entire life, and she became the same way herself. Out with petitions or at demonstrations or handing out leaflets—always involved in an important political cause. And she is handing this down to her kids. But Joe said his mother and father did not have anything they fanatically believed in. No central great cause. Nothing like the way Joe has lived his adult life. So the change—no, it was more truly not a change but a becoming—from Drifting Joe into Relentless Joe was still a long way off.

But it was always in Joe. In early tests they ask if you want to play in the orchestra or be the conductor. Do you want to play on the football team or do you want to be the quarterback? To those kinds of questions, Joe says he always answered, "conductor" and "quarterback." I believe that. Somewhere underneath his soft appearance was this desire to lead. He wasn't the leader of his group in grade school or middle school or high school or in the seminary. When he became a parish priest he loved the mission of Martin Luther King and the Social Justice Gospel and he started becoming more decisive. Till then he admits he had been sort of going along in life, dreaming, but drifting.

From Joe's letters to Sam

Dear Sam,

When you were in high school at Holy Angels you told me that you never saw or heard of a student there with hard drugs or even marijuana. I had a similar antiseptic experience during my high school years at Fenwick 40 years earlier. But there were a few uncomfortable memories.

I had a friend named Buddy Reynolds. Ours was an odd friendship. Bud was a star halfback for our championship football team. In fact, when I saw him recently he said he still holds the record for the longest punt in the Chicago area conference play. I remember the kick—it soared in a perfect arc, hit the ground, and rolled and rolled, and rolled. Buddy's thighs were powerful as locomotives, but his calf muscles jutted out at almost a 90-degree angle—sounds grotesque, but his legs were beautiful in a Popeye sort of way.

All irrelevant facts for what I want to tell you about Buddy and me. One weekend night, after a movie and pizza, Buddy and another suburban friend were driving me home. Now I had been to Buddy's house several times. He lived in one of those stately tan brick homes in a beautiful area of Oak Park, famous for its many Frank Lloyd Wright-designed houses. Each home stood on a substantial lot, had a driveway with a two-car garage and the home seemed to say in a dignified way, "This family has made it."

Well, as Bud drove down my street, Division Street, in the city of Chicago, the contrast between our living situations embarrassed me. I lived on a commercial street with streetcars and stores. He lived on a residential street with trees and lawns. I lived above my dad's awning shop; he lived in a two-story, 5-bedroom semi-mansion.

When he asked for specific directions to my home I said, "Why don't you just drop me off at this Austin Bowl, I can walk from there?"

"No, I don't mind. Where do you live?" he said.

After a couple more volleys I saw I wasn't getting anywhere—he was curious to see my exact residence. I got uncomfortable.

"That's O.K." I said. "I'm not ready to go home yet."

"Hey, where do you live? I just want to drop you off," he insisted.

The thoughts were running through my head—would he look down on me because my family didn't have the kind of money his family had? Would he think I was "low class"? Would our differences, if now revealed, affect our friendship?

The tension grew thick when I realized that Buddy was not going to let me off at the bowling alley and I realized that I couldn't lie and have him drop me off by the richest house on the block. In fact there were no "rich houses" on the block. I bit the bullet and said 5443 Division St. He quietly looked out his window at the addresses and drove slowly to my dad's shop. As soon as the car stopped I got out quickly, yelled, "See ya Monday," and hustled along the side of my building to get in the back door.

We never talked about that night, but our differences didn't affect our friendship, thanks to Buddy's good character.

I think of that night often, even now in my mid-60s when I'm at a party meeting new people and the question comes up as to where I live. Now I wear it as a badge of honor that I live in the inner city. I have a devilish curiosity as I wait to see the reaction of a wealthy Wayzata or Edina couple when I tell them I live a half mile south of the old Honeywell Headquarters in South Minneapolis.

If they seem shocked, I tend to write them off as good conservatives, but not the kind of people I'd want as friends.

But I still have my same old character flaw. If they are the kind of people I would like to think well of me, I somehow manage to work into the conversation that I live there by *choice*—it's part of my work—part of who I am. I'm not there because I'm poor, without options and without the talent to get out if I wanted to. I'm there to help improve the neighborhood and not avoid the problem.

Somehow I've not grown-up enough not to care about some people's approval. I'll probably die with that imperfection, but what the hell, it's better than being a serial killer or rapist, if only just barely. Ah, hubris; it doesn't let us rest.

'Night. Love,

Dad

P.S. You're at an age when you're sensitive about the image others have of you. Or maybe the approval of others is natural at any age. Even though it may sound hokey, read Kipling's poem "If." It's a helpful guide.

3. Justice Is in the Eye of the Beholder

Reflections on *Joe,* a play written for the Great American History Theatre, Saint Paul, MN

by Rev. Ed Flahavan

One day in the late 1960s, University of Minnesota political science professor Dr. Mulford Q. Sibley said to me, "You Catholics don't realize what a 'treasure you have hidden in the field' with the *corpus* of modern Catholic social teaching. And the irony is that I, a Quaker, am teaching probably the most complete course on that material in the Twin Cities in my Political Science classes at the University of Minnesota, a 'godless institution' in the estimation of some church people."

Sad to say, he was correct, of course. On both counts. Catholics by and large did not know their own church's social teachings. And that was largely true, I think, because Catholic education had pretty much backed away from presenting those teachings as Catholic population groups rose in social and economic circles.

Those teachings constitute the core of what we called a Catholic education. They trace their origin to the 1891 document "Rerum Novarum," ("On the Condition of Labor") by Pope Leo XIII, and continue in subsequent, progressively explicit documents right up to that night of Mulford Sibley's remarks.

If it were possible to summarize over 110 years of this continuously growing body of social doctrine, which it is not, I would dare to say that it rests on a platform supported by six pillars:

1. The options for the poor and vulnerable: The moral test of a society is how its most vulnerable are faring; their needs must come first.

2. The call to family, community, and participation: A central test of political, legal, and economic institutions is what they do TO people, what they do FOR people, and how people PARTICIPATE in them.

3. The life and dignity of the human person: People are more important than things because each person has dignity that comes from God, not social position, race, gender, age or economic status.

4. The rights and responsibilities of the human person: Flowing from this dignity, each person has rights, e.g. to freedom of conscience and religious liberty, to live free from unfair discrimination, and to have a share of earthly goods sufficient for oneself and one's family. At the same time each person has responsibilities, e.g. to one another, to the larger society, and to work for the common good.

5. The dignity of work and the rights of workers: In Catholic teaching, the economy exists to serve people, not the other way around.

6. Solidarity: Violent conflict and the denial of dignity and rights to people anywhere on the globe diminishes each of us.

When Joe Selvaggio and I trained for the Catholic priesthood in the 1950s and '60s, those documents were staple stuff of our training. They were part of the curriculum's "non-negotiable" required courses.

But things changed, especially as upward mobility lifted the Catholic descendants of immigrants out of poverty. Today, sad to say, it is a rare Catholic high school, college, seminary or university that requires the reading and study of those documents in full-blown, accredited courses.

Where does the person interested in learning more about this body of teaching find it?

One place to look is into the life and work of people who have been shaped so deeply by that teaching that they never have been the same thereafter. This is true not just of Catholics, of course, but of any person who has been grabbed by a lofty ethical system or religion. These people translate the best teachings of the world's religions—Jewish, Christian, Muslim or other—into action where they live and work. When they do so in an outstanding way, they attract admiration and attention—and imitation.

And so it has happened with Joe Selvaggio. He was largely shaped by his religious tradition, moved by it in a definite direction, not defeated by various obstacles placed in his way, nor deflected from his constant movement onward and upward. And so now we can "read" that story—in watching this play, *Joe.*

For those people—Catholic or otherwise—who wish to look more deeply and seriously at the Catholic social teachings that shaped Joe Selvaggio, and that Mulford Sibley referenced to me that evening, I recommend the resource called the Office for Social Justice of the Archdiocese of St. Paul and Minneapolis. You can find them at 328 W. Kellogg Boulevard, St. Paul, MN 55102; 651-291-4477.

Best of all, their Web site *(www.osjspm.org)* unwraps for you the very contents of that "treasure hidden in the field."

Rev. Ed Flahavan is a Roman Catholic priest and social justice advocate.

From Joe's letters to Sam:

Dear Sam,

Life can be dotted with ethical dilemmas that have their roots in ambiguity. And the results may haunt us in unexpected ways.

Among the memories that give me the most pleasure in my reflective aging years are the good times we shared when you were growing up and we went to Tuesday night movies.

Tuesdays were $1 nights, and we could get the whole family in at a cost I could afford. Even though we saw a great number of trashy movies, they served the relationship between you, your brothers Rick and Tony, and me well.

Last night I went to a movie alone. Vacations are great times to catch up on movies, and to have a beer or glass of wine. (In my old age, alcohol drains my energy too much while I'm working.) The movie was *Beijing Bicycle*. It was a story about two 17-year-old Chinese boys who both thought they had a legitimate claim to the same bicycle. The movie reminded me of a similar story from my own youth, involving my friend "Cos."

Cos and I were in about seventh or eighth grade. We and about five to ten other guys were pretty close friends—playing on the same ball teams, going to Our Lady Help of Christians grammar school, and chasing the girls together. One afternoon some of the "gang" decided we wanted to see a big NBA game that was coming up. We saved our shekels and made plans to go down to Chicago Stadium to buy tickets a few weeks before the game.

For some reason Cos couldn't go to the Stadium to purchase the tickets that Saturday. I volunteered to purchase his ticket if he'd give me the money. He promptly gave me about $5.00—the price, those days, for a young fan. The other three or four of us got up early one Saturday, met, took a bus and then an "El," and walked through a "scary" neighborhood over to Madison Avenue.

When we got to the ticket office, we were shocked to find out that the ticket price had risen to about $7.50 from the $5.00 we expected. What to do? We really wanted to go to the game. We didn't want to return home to see if we could borrow the extra money from our parents, so someone had the clever idea of trying to beg for the money from the adult sports fans who were coming to buy tickets. They wouldn't miss another 50 cents or so. If we could each find a few generous souls, we'd be able to hit the $7.50 ticket price and return home, mission accomplished.

We stood on the sidewalk in front of the huge Stadium saying, "Sir, I traveled all the way from the far West Side to buy tickets to the big game, but they went and raised the price of the tickets on us. Would you happen to have an extra 50 cents to help me buy a ticket?" It was tough, embarrassing work, but after an hour or so we were all able to raise the extra money. I had it tougher than the rest of the guys since I not only had to raise my extra money, but Cos's too. But after we were done, we were all pretty pleased with ourselves.

That afternoon when I gave the ticket to Cos and showed him the ticket price I sheepishly asked him for the extra $2.50. "What do you mean?" asked Cos. "You got the money for free from other fans."

"Sure, but it wasn't easy," I protested. "It was hard work. And it was humiliating."

"Tough titty," was Cos's firm reply. "I'm not paying for something you got free—especially when I didn't ask you to do it."

"But everyone thought you'd want me to beg for you," I continued.

"Don't be ridiculous," Cos shot back.

I could see I was getting nowhere, so I dropped the subject. But to this day I feel that a fair judge would have told Cos to pay me the extra money—or at least half of it.

Here's where the movie comes in. The one Chinese boy, who had worked very hard as a messenger to earn this beautiful new bike, had it stolen. He was determined to get it back. Since he put a distinguishing small scratch on it, he knew he'd recognize it. The only problem was that there were tens of thousands—maybe millions—of bikes in Beijing.

But, because it was a movie, he beat the odds and found the bike in the possession of an upper-class 17-year-old student. When confronted by the boy the student said, "I bought this bike from a used bike shop. I can't help it if you used to own it. I am the rightful owner now."

Since the messenger boy sensed the student was firm in his will to keep the bike, the messenger boy wrestled the bike away and took off. Later on, the student got some of his friends to try to get the bike away from the messenger. The friends cornered the messenger at a construction site, but he was so tenacious in holding onto the bike that, after several hours, when they were all tired, the student's friends got the messenger to agree to share the bike—each one getting the bike every other day. It was a kind of "Solomon-like" solution that worked fairly well. I won't tell you more in case you want to see the movie.

But my point is fairly obvious. We either need "Solomon-like" judges around to enforce decisions, or we need one party to give in the way I did with Cos. Otherwise disputes just keep escalating, whether the parties are fighting over $2.50, a bike, or geography around Jerusalem.

I'd ask Cos what he thinks, but he went on to the next life.

Curiously, the law has an answer to the bike problem—an owner never loses title to a stolen item, so the richer boy had no right to the bike, no matter that he bought it believing the transaction was a valid one.

Most people don't like the concept of one side "giving in." But I think that's mostly what has to happen. One side says, "Let it go." The South said it after the Civil War. Germany and Japan said it after World War II. The U. S. said it after we lost the Vietnam War. But the Irish and the English haven't said it. The Israelis and the Palestinians haven't yet said it. And the fighting goes on. It's one of the painful truisms of life that the solution to these conflicts will inevitably involve everyone's emerging at least somewhat dissatisfied with the results.

Love,

Dad

4. Forks in the Road: Decision Time

Life's Crucial Intersections

by Tony Bouza

Life is change. Each of us encounters crossroads on the journey. Which fork to take? Retrospect offers the best perspective, only it's too late then. Adopting a sound set of principles, embracing sensible values, and exercising a mercilessly introspective mien offer the best chances for a satisfying outcome. And these crucial intersections probably occur no oftener than four or five times in a lifetime.

From Joe's letters to Sam

Dear Sam,

You and your cell phone! I have this image of you walking around New York and L.A. with this damn phone in your ear. Lots of young people do it. Not only in La La Land or the Big Apple, but in Manila, Minneapolis, and Fort Wayne, Indiana. I won't criticize it, because it's not part of my culture. But I do want to tell you about 5 phone calls that were not the casual kinds of calls you get all day long. These were serious, life-altering calls I got at different stages of my life.

And, maybe, there *really* are only five *important* calls in anyone's life.

The *first* phone call that gave me a fork in the road was a call I received at Marquette University in Milwaukee in September of 1955. It came during my first year of college—in the middle of registration week. My older brother John was on the line and he said, "Peppe," (short for Giuseppe, the name he called me in my younger days) "you've got to stop your registration in Business Administration and register in Engineering instead."

"Engineering?" I responded. "What for? I have no interest in being an engineer. I'm just going to take over Dad's awning business."

"It doesn't matter. The math and science you'll get in engineering will help you think more clearly, so even if you take over Dad's business, you'll be sharper, and a better awning man for it," he said with a determined voice.

This was around the time the Russians had sent up the first space satellite, Sputnik, and engineers were suddenly getting enormous respect. Even with the respect I had for both the engineers and my brother's opinion, I thought this call was awfully intrusive. Today I think of it as even more intrusive. But back then, a younger brother in an Italian family was supposed to trust his brother's advice, and that I did—switching into engineering for the next three years, and studying more math and science than I care to think about.

• • •

The *second* influential phone call I received came in the early spring of my junior year, 1958. This time the call was from my mother. "Joey," (another name from my youth) she said, "your father had a stroke. He's in the hospital and can't run the business." I could tell from her shaky voice that she needed help.

"I don't know—I really don't know what to do," she quivered. She didn't ask me to drop out of college to come home to run the family business, but it seemed like my only choice.

Based on the fear in her voice and the gravity of the situation I knew I had better go home right away. I did, and it lasted three weeks, since my dad recovered well enough to resume running the business. But during those three weeks I learned that I didn't want to run an awning shop.

I started to think about my career, and a vocation to the priesthood entered my consideration. I decided to call a priest at my old high school, Fr. Jacobs, whose judgment I trusted, and I asked him if there was a monastery or some other place I could go to think about my future and the possibility of my becoming a priest. He told me there was and said that as a matter of fact, there happened to be a retreat for young men considering the priesthood, coming up at a remote monastery. His suggestion had an immediate appeal to me, so I signed up for the retreat. I was able to return to finish my junior year at Marquette U, but, during a weekend in May of that year, I found myself at the retreat led by a very charismatic provincial vocation director from Chicago, Fr. Gilbert Graham, who led me to a decision to enter the Dominican Order. I studied Latin intensely over the summer and found myself entering the Novitiate on August 4th—St. Dominic's Day—and, 10 days later, being invested in my white habit and black cappa and taking a one-year promise of chastity. Quite a change for a guy who had been chasing the girls at Marquette three months earlier.

• • •

The *third* call came ten years later. It was 1965, at the height of the civil rights movement. Big German Shepherd police dogs were biting the Blacks who were trying to vote, and the powerful streams from the fire hoses were knocking down men women and children who were protesting for their God-given rights. Most of us in the seminary wanted to go down to Selma and other southern towns to put our newly found Christian principles into practice to help this great new preacher, Martin Luther King, Jr. But we were stuck *studying* those principles up in Dubuque, Iowa.

Then one day one of my professors, a Fr. Horse Hunter, nicknamed "Horse" because of his bulky size, put his arm on my shoulder and said, "Brother Anthony," (this was in my Brother Anthony or Brother Tony stage, when I was known by the religious name given to me) "I know of your intense interest in the civil rights movement, so I need you to sit by the phone today, all day if necessary. Martin

Luther King, Jr. will be calling for me, but I can't be available. You've got to take the call and convince him to meet briefly next week, when he's in Chicago, with our Master General, who will also be in Chicago. You've got to convince King that our Master General is this 'big-shot' from Rome, and that a picture of the two of them together could help generate greater support from the Catholic community for King's civil rights movement. Tell him the photo has a good chance of getting picked up by the wire services, and it could give him international exposure with the Catholic community."

I didn't need any persuading. I was thrilled to sit at a phone calling King's secretary every hour to remind her of the importance of this call. The secretary kept assuring me that she would call King at his earliest opportunity as he traveled from town to town across Mississippi and Louisiana.

Sure enough, the call came, and I found myself on the phone with my great Christian idol, trying to suppress my nervousness and acting important. During the five to seven minutes of tense dialogue I mustered up my strongest arguments, and King responded in his distinctive baritone voice, until finally, lo and behold, he agreed to meet with our Master General the next week. I was ecstatic—almost skipping down the hall bursting to tell Fr. Horse Hunter and my classmates the great news.

The bottom line on this third phone call was mixed. The conservatives got to our Master General and talked him out of meeting with MLK, because King was too "radical." But an equally important bottom line for me, I think, was that it solidified my desire to serve as a Martin Luther King-type minister, working with the poor for social justice. Because of that call I asked to be assigned to a poor parish, with minorities, and was granted my wish with an assignment to Holy Rosary parish in South Minneapolis.

• • •

My *fourth* phone call came in 1968 during my "Father Joe" stage—after two years as a parish priest at Holy Rosary.

First, some background. After my first year there, my pastor had accused me of being more interested in the "social-work ministry" of the civil rights and peace movements than in the sacramental ministries. I was heavily involved in the war on poverty, protested at Hubert Humphrey's visit to the Guthrie when he was the big defender of our policy in Vietnam, and had a sign in my window that said, "Stop white racism." The pastor in 1967 even tried to get me transferred to a pastor out in Louisiana nicknamed "Crusher Connelly," who would be better equipped to rein in this aggressive young priest. Fortunately, due to the effective organizing of a parishioner, Marie Manthey, who organized the youth club, the women of the Third Order of St. Dominic, the men in the Holy Name Society, and local politicians, I was able to stay. But that's another long story, which I'll tell you in a letter about the "arc" of my life.

After the second year, which was more turbulent than the first, since Martin Luther King was assassinated in April, and Bobby Kennedy in August, I was even more involved and interested in the "Secular Issues" as my pastor would call them. So much so that I decided to call Fr. Graham, who was now my Provincial, to talk over my situation. The phone call that Friday morning went something like this.

"Fr. Graham, this is Joe Selvaggio calling from Holy Rosary. I hope you are well, but I have some serious thoughts to talk over with you. You know of my burning interests in the civil rights and peace movements, but now I'm starting to have doubts about other aspects of the priesthood. I have trouble with the Church's position on divorce and remarriage, birth control, and then there's this woman I met."

As soon as I mentioned the word *woman*—about 30 seconds into the conversation—he suspended me and told me he thought it best that I just leave as soon as possible.

I did, and I was out of the building with $5 to my name the next day, a Saturday morning. I remember a lawyer telling me, "They can't kick you out that fast. You have solemn vows. You're ordained. That's your family. I'll take your case pro bono." But I said, "No thanks. It's probably for the best." I may not have had the courage to be so decisive. Even though I loved the Dominican Community a great deal, I thought the "activist community" was even more the place where I belonged. It was the '60s, when radical decisions were much admired.

• • •

The *fifth* and final phone call came about 15 years later. My marriage broke up after 13 years, so I was single again, living with my two adopted 16-year-old boys, Ricardo and Antonio, and a 16-year-old-foster son, Minh. As you'll recall, Sam, you were living with your mother, but we saw each other twice a week. Before I got the fifth call, I got a letter from an old college classmate, Fr. Bob McCahill who was now a Maryknoll Missionary in Bangladesh. The essence of his letter was something like this: "Joe, a family in the Philippines I know well from the 15 years I spent there has a problem. One of the daughters, a 35-year-old woman, has had to go underground because of her aggressive opposition to President Ferdinand Marcos. She got called in for questioning, and, rather than face possible torture, rape, and even death, she decided to go "underground" and be a communicator between the rebels in the hills and the activists in the cities. She used to be a teacher, and her family would love to get her out of the country. Her brother is a lawyer and could arrange to get her a fiancé visa if I know of someone who would marry her—just for a short time—maybe six months or a year. After that time the INS should not be suspicious if there was a divorce, and the ordeal would be over."

He didn't ask me directly if I'd marry her, but I thought, what the heck, I've got a girlfriend, but we can't get married until my older boys and her two girls finished high school, two years from now. The Filipina and I could live as "brother and sister," and she'll get helped with little trouble to anyone. So I volunteered.

Since I didn't have any money at the time, I got some of my friends to kick in $700 to $900 for a plane ticket and we threw a little welcoming party for her at the Carmichael-Lynch (formerly the Pillsbury) mansion where I was able to introduce her to several members of the Filipino community here in Minneapolis. This was in February. By the first of June I was starting to have problems with my girlfriend, so we decided to take a month-long break to see if our relationship was strong enough to continue. On Saturday morning, June 30th, as I had promised to do, I called my girlfriend.

I can remember this fifth call, about 19 years later, as if it were yesterday. Within seconds my girlfriend said, "Well, are you still living as 'brother and sister' with your wife, or did you consummate the marriage?" At that moment I knew I had already chosen one of the two paths leading from the present fork in the road. I was now really married to Rose Escañan, and my relationship with my girlfriend was over. I had to repay the airfare money to my friends, since I was now in a real marriage. In early March of 2004 we will have been married for 20 years.

• • •

So what's the point of telling you about all these forks in the road with momentous consequences? Do I have any wisdom to offer? Can I recommend choosing the more risky path for more happiness? Can I urge you to opt for safety and cover your bottom rather than chose adventure? I really can't. I think there are no simple answers. Sometimes risks will bring you happiness. Other times safety is the best course.

Although I have no sure-fire formula to help with your big decisions—or even with the hundreds of decisions you'll be making every day, I do have a couple of thoughts, plus one very important resource.

The first thought comes from Aristotle. He said, when you have an important decision to make, and you don't know which way to go, ask some wise people what they think. Ask those who have had some experience in life and seem to have their heads screwed on right. That process will give you your best chance of a good decision.

I would add a second thought to Aristotle's: When you make the decision, make it with others in mind—not just your own selfish interests. That way, when you look back, you'll be able too say, "Well, it may have been the wrong choice, but I did it for the right reason. I did my best."

But the most important thought I have to leave you with is this *resource* idea. And this is where St. Joan of Arc comes in—not the person, but the parish. A parish like this one, with its motto "We welcome you wherever you are in your journey," can be a tremendous help to you. I've been attending St. Joan's from the first mass in the gym—through my leaving the priesthood, getting married, getting divorced, getting married again, working with the poor at Project for Pride in Living, and now working with the rich at The One Percent Club. All along my journey, my hard journey, because life is hard for all of us, this family—the smiling faces at these Sunday Masses, the energizing and inspiring music, and the small Christian communities, whether formal or just friends—was there for me as I faced those decisions.

About 2000 years ago a famous saying, "Civus Romanus sum," or "I am a Roman citizen," was the proud claim of all those associated with Rome. Today, as I think of going to St. Joan of Arc, I think the saying should be, "Soy miembro de la parroquia de Santa Juana de Arco"—I am a member of St. Joan of Arc parish.

I hope you are able to find an equally supportive community as you travel through life. If you can't find it in a church, perhaps you can find it in friends, family, or a "spirituality group."

And, beware. That cell phone of yours could give you some life-changing calls.

Love,

Dad

5. Faith and Reason

From the play *Joe*

Mother Church sent Joe places where he began to see people very unlike the family that he grew up in. Mother Church gave Joe real life experiences to go with the philosophy he was hearing from the outside world. That was primarily Martin Luther King, Jr., but also the rest of the Rap From Our Time. Civil Rights. The Vietnam War. Justice… Peace. What makes it all come together for Joe is the every day experience he is getting working in these different places and meeting the people there. Working in different worlds than the one he grew up in. And it was Mother Church that sent him out to get these experiences and help further his changing. And in Joe's case it is apt to call it Mother Church because the Catholic Church helped give birth to the New Joe. The Joe who was well on his way to becoming Relentless Joe.

The Church helped to change him. to give him discipline and a first rate education. His education in Mother Church exposed Joe to what he calls, "great ideas and great thoughts." The Church started him on a line of changes that would one day include leaving Mother Church. To being reborn outside The Church for the first time in his life. But, in one of life's little ironies, Joe couldn't have gotten to the point of figuring out how and why to essentially leave Mother Church without the education in school and in life that Mother Church gave him. Martin Luther had the same experience.

From Joe's letters to Sam:

Dear Sam,

My mother was a faith-oriented person. She always ended her announced plans with, "God willing." When I was in the seminary there was a lovable scripture scholar named Benedict "Benoit" Viviano, who used to say, "Our faith is not superstition. Sometimes those little old ladies in Mexico, although Catholic, slip into superstition. Their minds are still influenced by their former Mayan religiosity. We in North America don't have that historical pagan superstition to overcome."

While I respected Benoit's opinion, I could never figure out how one could tell if one's faith was tainted with superstition (like the Mexican woman's) or pure like my devout North American mother's. In my early years, I was a person of strong faith. When I was trying to figure out whether or not to go into the priesthood, my faith told me I *should* go, celibacy and all. I knew it did not make much sense rationally, but my faith told me that I'd be "saving souls." What could be more important than that? And for my important work, I would get rewarded eternally, with a very high place in heaven.

Coming from a strong faith background, I can understand the mentality of the suicide bombers behind 9/11. They were fighting the great Satan and about to get rewarded with 77 adoring virgins in heaven. Forty years ago I thought of getting martyred by the godless communists but would get rewarded through eternal happiness in heaven. If we Catholics would have had the "adoring virgins" in our sacred scriptures, I'm sure vocations to the priesthood would have quadrupled. (Future revisers of the Bible, take note.)

In the seminary we were taught that faith and reason are never in real contradiction. Faith goes *beyond* reason. Both are forms of knowledge. Reason can bring us knowledge by everyday evidence—one plus one is two…if we are not nourished by food and water, we will get hungry and die. All civilizations throughout the world accept these truths as self-evident, or deduced from logic. But faith, on the other hand, is a gift from God. We were taught that while there is strong evidence that God exists, we cannot definitively prove that God exists. We need *faith* to give us certitude. Sure we can use reason to argue that it doesn't make sense for this world to be here. Something can't come from nothing. An all-powerful creator, whom we'll call God, must have created our world. Or, we can argue that all the order, beauty and intelligence itself cries out as evidence that a superior intelligence (whom we call God) must have always existed prior to our beauty and intelligence. Again, reasonable arguments, but not conclusive. To really be sure God exists, we need the knowledge (aided by an act of the will, according to Aquinas) coming from the gift of faith.

Now that I'm older I'm having trouble with what I was taught. The following e-mail joke I received recently crystallizes my uneasiness with faith.

Joke: An elderly Jewish man was praying at the Wailing Wall. A journalist across the street was watching from his hotel and said to the concierge, "Tell me about that man."

The concierge said, "Oh, he's been praying like that for 25 years—morning, noon, and night."

"Really?" replied the journalist. "That's impressive. I'd love to talk to him."

"Go ahead. He's very friendly."

The journalist proceeded across the street and said to the man, "Excuse me, sir, would you tell me about your prayer life?"

"Well," the Jew replied, "in the morning I pray that the Israelis and the Palestinians stop their fighting and solve their problems non-violently; in the afternoon I pray for world peace…the Indians stop fighting with the Pakistanis or the Irish with the English…and in the evening I pray the world prospers with the elimination of poverty, disease, and hunger."

"Wow!" said the journalist in awe. "Twenty five years!! How does that make you *feel*?"

The Jew thought for a moment and answered, "It makes me feel like I'm talking to a f___ing wall."

My atheist friends tell me he *was* talking to a wall.

My mother prayed all her life that God would take her before she had to go into a nursing home. Two years before she died, I had to put her in a nursing home.

Are these stories unanswered prayers of faithful people? Are they answered, but not the answers the faithful wanted to hear? Or is there a God out there who doesn't intervene in our world? Or is there simply no God out there at all?

Who knows? I submit no one knows. I like the fact that the Catholic Church teaches that we cannot know with certainty through reason alone, that God even exists.

I like the fact that the Church teaches "the supremacy of conscience." That's all we have when you come right down to it. We must be true to our conscience or we are lying to ourselves. When our conscience is telling us something is true, or is not true, or we just don't know, we should be comfortable with that. We shouldn't try to change our opinion because we fear God will punish us or we'll lose our eternal life. If we define God as an honest loving God, he/she would want us to be honest—to assent to whatever we see the truth to be.

Right now, I see the truth to be "I don't know." If that makes me an agnostic and my friends are unhappy with me, so be it. That's the way I see it. That's the way I'll call it. The wisest minds have always said that there is a need to question—that life is a search.

My friend Benoit will be disappointed with me. I know, because he said he was very sad, worried, and upset with his nephew who had declared himself an atheist. "How can you be disappointed with him when you hold to "the supremacy of conscience?" I asked Benoit. He was unmoved by my thoughts on the subject.

Love ya,

Dad

P. S. A poll sponsored by the Washington-based Pew Research Center for the People and the Press found that 59 percent of Americans thought religion was important while the percentages in other developed countries was significantly lower—Italy (27), Germany (21), Japan (12), and France (11). The poll reminded me of Thomas Jefferson's prediction that religion in the U.S. would fade to just about nothing in 200 years. He was almost right about the rest of the wealthy nations, but wrong about the U.S.

Dear Sam,

Remember Fr. Bob McCahill? He's the wiry Maryknoll missionary priest from Bangladesh. Bob and I went to Marquette University together. He departed to Maryknoll about a year before I went off to the Dominicans. I have a great deal of respect for Bob. He lives in a bamboo hut he built for $30 worth of materials. His floor is mother earth, and his morning coffee container is a tin cup disturbingly similar to those used by the street beggars.

Bob is in Bangladesh living a life of simplicity and service. He doesn't try to convert the Muslims—he simply tries to show them that Christians can be good people, too. Jesus lived a simple life and served the poor—not the powerful. Bob is there to do what Jesus would do today: live simply, serve the poor.

Every morning, after his cup of coffee and a long meditation, Bob gets on his bicycle, rides along until he sees a very sick person, and asks that person if he would like to be transported to a hospital to see what the doctors can do for him. The forlorn individual will usually say, "I can't afford a hospital." Bob tells the man not to worry—there will be no expense. Bob has a deal with the hospitals. They will accept so many of Bob's "carry-ins" per week, for no charge. Bob will pick them up when the hospital is ready to release them. No arguments, no money exchanges. That's the deal. Bob's been doing this in about 6 different villages within 50 miles of Dacca for over 20 years now.

Bob would say his *faith* brought him to perform his unusual kind of service. This kind of faith produces service and good works. Even if there is no God and no reward for Bob's kind of actions, it still makes sense. That's what St. Theresa of Avila told God once when she was at prayer. If Bob is wrong about his faith, people still were helped who would not have been helped without his efforts.

But I now differ from Bob on his great respect for the Muslim faith (or any faith, for that matter). The Muslims are all going around saying "Allah willing. It was the will of Allah." It wasn't the will of Allah that all those innocent people died on 9/11. It's not the will of Allah that little Taysha, an 11 year old girl got shot and killed by a stray bullet fired by a stupid gang member in our neighborhood last week. It's not the will of Allah that those thousands of people were killed or made homeless in the latest floods in Bangladesh. Those tragedies happen—whether from acts of nature or from acts emanating from our ignorant human nature. Allah has nothing to do with it, and we should quit giving religions, whether Muslim, Jewish, or Christian, the power to explain it to us.

After 9/11 I think former president Bill Clinton had the wisest words to say. While all of the commentaries were trying to figure out how to understand and respond to such a tragedy, Clinton said that we had to talk to the Muslim world about what we had in *common*—the earth, our humanity, our science, our logic and reason. Implied in his view is to leave faith out of it, because we don't have faith *in common*. Whenever you have a disagreement with someone, you should start by discussing points you have in common—points you agree upon. Then see if you can expand to other areas to agree upon. Faith, by definition, is something we do *not* have in common. Each religious faith thinks it has the revealed word of God. Consequently, God sees things pretty close to the way that religion sees them. This has gotten the world in a whole heap of trouble.

Bishop Desmond Tutu of South Africa once answered someone who was criticizing religion because it caused disharmony and even wars by saying, “Religion should be thought of as morally neutral—just as a knife can be used to cut butter or a man’s stomach, religion can be used for good or evil.”

It’s my understanding that Thomas Jefferson tried to re-write the New Testament without all the miracles and dogmas. He viewed the New Testament as an advanced ethical piece of writing written by the wisest men of their times. Personally, I think Jefferson took some of those wise concepts and improved upon them with the Declaration of Independence. Later the Supreme Court and Congress improved the Constitution by adding amendments like the one abolishing slavery.

To think that the “sacred scriptures” have all the answers for all time makes no sense to me. Just spend some time reading them and you’ll see that they have some strange views, with firmaments beyond the skies and heavens, and God demanding human sacrifice to assuage His wrath. Even slavery and loaning your wife to a traveler are seen in some instances as morally fine.

One author who helped the scales fall from my eyes was Joseph Campbell. Campbell said that the only gospel that contained the Virgin birth was Luke’s gospel, and that was because Luke was a Greek. Greeks always had virgin births in their mythologies.

“What?” I thought. “The virgin birth was there because of the pagan myths, not because God made it happen?” Some of my faith, or better yet, my superstitions began to crumble. I came back to the question I asked myself 40 years ago when Benoit tried to distinguish faith from superstition. Then, I was reluctant to doubt anything taught in the scriptures or in the seminary. I was afraid I’d lose my faith. Now, I’m reluctant to believe anything I can’t prove by science, math, or logic. Now I’m afraid I’m being superstitious rather than rational. And therein lies the heart of one conflict between the parishioners of St. Joan of Arc and Rome.

Earlier this year an Iranian professor was arrested for telling his students that Islam needs a “Protestant Reformation—to bring the scriptures’ interpretations into modernity. He was immediately put on death row. I think he’s 100 percent right. I don’t hold out much hope that a reform movement will change the fundamentalist Muslims much, but it will help the world. The Protestant Reformation didn’t change the Vatican much, but it certainly helped the world by creating a much more decentralized, tolerant, and diverse Christianity.

I know Muslims who think for themselves. The world needs more of them. Unfortunately the religions that are growing are the fundamentalist ones—whether Christian, Islamic, or Jewish. God save us from these nuts.

Reason is king with me now. If I can't reason it out with logic or scientific proof I say, "Maybe, maybe not." (While in my heart feeling "probably not.")

Now I feel intellectually honest. Let people believe what they want, but let's not bring faith into public policy. It's no wonder our founding parents separated church and state.

Love,

Dad

6. Spiritual Nourishment

From the play *Joe*

I remember that, to us Protestants, the Rev. Bishop Fulton J. Sheen was like Batman. No really. This guy came sweeping into a room wearing a cape. A cape. Listen, where I grew up, only Batman could wear a cape and get away with it. So to us Protestants this guy was like Batman. Here was one of "Them"—meaning Catholics—who was white. I grew up on the border between Texas and Mexico, where it was a given that all Catholics were Mexicans and all white people were Protestants. But here was a white Catholic in a comic book costume. So we would watch a few minutes out of raw curiosity and then we would make fun of the guy for a couple of minutes and then we would get bored and switch channels to the live broadcast of the bullfights from Mexico City. But back at Joe's house they were still watching Bishop Sheen. Everybody in Joe's family watched it—even Joe's father.

The Journey Continues

by Rev. George Wertin

Joe has been an integral part of the Church of St. Joan of Arc in South Minneapolis since before there was a Project for Pride in Living. In fact, PPL's roots are at St. Joan of Arc. In those days, Harvey Egan was pastor. He had inaugurated "the gym liturgies" with their lively music and focus on outreach into the world. There was a strong bond of solidarity among members of the community. Joe was struggling. He had a vision, but few resources. It was in the conversations after Mass that the parishioners searched for a way to sustain Joe and his new ministry. It was through pledges of ten and twenty dollars a month by a core group of parishioners that Joe was able to find a modicum of financial stability so that he could build a foundation for his dream.

Joe continues to be a committed member of St. Joan of Arc. The motto of St. Joan of Arc parish is, "We welcome you wherever you are on your journey." That fits Joe well. He appreciates the parish's commitment to equality for women and naming God as Mother as well as Father. He also endorses the parish's pledge to be a peace church working for non-violent solutions to conflict. And he supports the church's visible presence in the larger community.

Parishioners appreciate it when Joe gives the sermon at the Sunday gym liturgies, as he does on an occasional basis. His approach is typically low-key. He always begins with a humorous story that ends up making a point. There is a gentle chuckle that ripples through the congregation as Joe continues sharing his experiences. Recently he has drawn on his travels to Haiti, Cuba and the Philippines. He reveals his compassion for poor people. He doesn't lay a guilt trip on people. Rather he shares how he himself responds to people living in poverty. His vulnerability allows others to explore how they too can make a difference in the world.

Perhaps the most remarkable achievement of Joe's career is that PPL moves on without him. It did not collapse when he moved on to start the One Percent Club. PPL has its own identity. Joe continues to be a cheerleader for PPL. But PPL has a life of its own. And Joe continues to be a gently abrasive force as he continues his journey.

Rev. George Wertin is pastor at St. Joan of Arc Catholic Church in South Minneapolis.

From Joe's letters to Sam:

Dear Sam,

St. Joan of Arc Parish—my spiritual well—is in controversy again. This time Archbishop Harry Flynn prevented giving a catechesis award to one of the designated 15 winners from the diocese—because she is a lesbian. The media has been playing up the story, and about 100 parishioners from the parish picketed the awards dinner.

The archbishop defended his actions in the diocesan paper by saying, "I could not, in conscience, commend someone for promoting that which is not harmonious with church doctrine. This is particularly true when that person's role, and the very reason for which she would have received the award, involves the teaching ministry of the church."

Was the catechist promoting lesbianism? Of course not. She was teaching Church doctrine, but not hiding her lesbianism. I think there's a difference. Does the archbishop think he can examine the personal lives of all people teaching Church doctrine and determine whether they are measuring up?

This archbishop seems hard-wired to Rome, and, if he's going to stay that way, there is no solution to this problem. I basically blame Rome. Pope John Paul II picked bishops who were very loyal, and now they are just "doing their job."

My preference is for bishops to think for themselves. Contrast this latest story with one that happened 20 or so years ago at the parish. Gloria Steinem, the well-known feminist and pro-choice advocate, spoke at St. Joan's. She was greeted outside the church by protesters with placards showing pictures of bloody fetuses that had been photographed after an abortion. Gloria gave her talk without mentioning abortion (a condition attached to the speaking engagement) and was given a long, standing ovation.

A couple of weeks later Archbishop John Roach called the pastor, Fr. Harvey Egan into his office and said to him (according to my reliable sources), "Harvey, I've got to reprimand you. The right-wingers are on my case and I've got to do something. I've drafted this letter to you. What do you think?"

Harvey looked at the letter and said, "John, you shouldn't talk to me this way."

The bishop responded, "Well, how should I talk to you?"

Harvey took his pen, crossed out several sentences, added a couple of new sentences, and slid the paper across the desk to the archbishop.

Roach looked at it and said, "O.K., I can live with this." And that was the resolution of the conflict. I've always felt that disagreements should be resolved that way. Each side saved face. Each side walked away feeling that it had won something.

But this present conflict (I predict) will not be done that way. Rome and this archbishop will win. St. Joan's will lose, and many liberal Catholics will vote with their feet and leave the church. The church will move toward being just another conservative Christian denomination rather than being the "big tent," (or big "corral," as archbishop Roach would have said), welcoming people wherever they are on their journey. The Church will be Catholic with a capital "C" but not with a small "c."

Gay sex, birth control, even abortion, are controversial moral issues. They should not be judged like murder, rape, and theft. When vast numbers of good people think some action is morally O.K., then large institutions like governments and churches should allow people to take that action and still be members.

Our views of morality have evolved over the ages, even as our abhorrence for murder, rape, incest and such has remained constant. This is the difference between prohibited acts and those seen as intrinsically and instinctively wrong and unacceptable. *Mala prohibitum* versus *mala in se.*

I like being a member of St. Joan's because its people are tolerant and always defend the rights of the "little guy." But I think I like it even more because it gives me spiritual nourishment. When I'm there I feel good. When I'm singing their songs tears will often emerge from my eyes. The other night I heard Bob Hope explain why he loves golf. He said, "It's healthy. You're out there in the fresh air—exercising all the parts of your body and mind—you take a shower and maybe have a massage. You feel great." That's the way I feel about St. Joan's. I still need my physical workout at the Minneapolis Club, but for my spiritual health, there's nothing like an hour-long Mass at St. Joan's.

Hope you find such a place. Hope it's in the Catholic Church, but now I feel it's more important to find such a place—whether it's in the Church or not.

Love,

Dad

7. Tolerance and Openness

Life Demands a Clear View

by Tony Bouza

Polarity is the foe of reason. A questioning mind may not produce certain answers, but it will assure the search needed to produce rational outcomes—which can themselves be tested. The Church's problem—and its durability—lie in its certitude about questions humans should agonize over. The role of women; homosexuality; religion and the state; the importance of ritual; the acceptance of dogma on faith are only a few of the troubling questions stirring the consciences of members who want desperately to believe. But blind belief is just that—blind. Life insists on an unblinkered look at the things around us.

From Joe's letters to Sam:

Dear Sam,

When I wrote my op-ed piece about recycled condoms, and asked priests and bishops who agreed with me to communicate their feelings to the Catholic Church hierarchy, one priest friend who had been courageous in fighting some Church policies in the past said, "My positions just threw a 'suspicion' on me. If I were to take up your call to be 'pro condom' I would be committing clerical career suicide. There is a whole list of issues. Some are above the line and some are below the line. Your position is certainly below the line."

I was intrigued. I don't spend much time thinking about those issues anymore since I am a member of St. Joan of Arc Parish—a Catholic parish in good standing with the Bishop, but a parish where "all are welcome wherever you are in your journey." You and I are on different journeys, but I know it's still important to both of us to consider ourselves Catholic. Since my priest friend didn't have a list of positions "above and below the line," I decided to try to make my own list.

Here's my off-the-top-of-my-head list of "approved," "suspicious," and "career-suicide" issues for the Catholic clergy:

Approved:

Complete assent to the teachings of Rome
Celibacy as a "higher state" than marriage
Baptism as necessary to gain heaven
Giving generously to the poor

Suspicious:

Women and married people should be ordained priests
Divorced and re-married Catholics should receive the sacraments
Some sex outside of marriage is O.K.
Complete pacifism (no war) is better than war

Career Suicide:

Promotion of condom use
Promotion of committed homosexual unions
The Pope is just one moral voice among many (not infallible)
Pro-choice (on the abortion issue)

Then I got to thinking about what Bill Cooper, the former head of Minnesota's Republican Party was saying when he called for fellow Republicans to answer a questionnaire designed to weed out all the party members who call themselves conservatives, but are really Democrats or liberals in disguise, in Cooper's opinion. Some Ralph Nader supporters also have litmus tests for the "true" liberal. Here are my Liberal and Conservative lists:

Liberal:

Approved:

Pro union
Pro safety net
Pro regulation
Pro environment

Suspicious:

Pro self-sufficiency
Pro marketplace
Pro nuclear family
Pro Super Patriotism

Suicide:

Pro large corporations
Pro small government and small government programs
Pro racial profiling
Pro life

Conservative:

Approved:

Pro free market
Pro nuclear family
Pro Law and Order
Pro Flag waving

Suspicious:

Pro Choice
Pro Progressive taxation
Pro Safety net
Pro Affirmative Action

Suicide:

Pro taxation and large government social programs
Pro Union
Pro heavy government regulation (especially gun control)
Pro permissive human behavior

I suppose someone who doesn't have lists could be accused of not having convictions. I like people with convictions. I just don't want them to throw me out of "the club" if my convictions happen to be different from their convictions. I consider myself a Catholic, an American, a liberal, and a conservative. But I resent having to accept every position associated with those labels.

You could argue that there should be a lot of "little clubs" with people whose members all agree with each other. The trouble with that thinking is that it would eliminate dialogue. It would prevent our learning from each other. As it is, if we consider ourselves conservative, we tend to just read other conservatives. If liberal, we listen mostly to liberals. I prefer some "big tents" so I can read and hear conflicting opinions. Dissent is a very useful commodity for an effective society. (I think this is the genius of our two-party system: both parties are "big tents.") I've always admired the German philosopher Hegel, who promoted dialogue so strongly that the process became known as "Hegelian dialectic." For example, Hegel would argue strongly for freedom. Then he would argue just as strongly for safety. After hearing both sides of the arguments, the listeners could reach a reasonable balance between freedom and safety.

If the Catholic Church had a free and open dialogue about celibacy, homosexuality, masturbation and other sexual issues, I believe it would have had less of a problem with child sexual abuse. Likewise, if Americans can have an open debate about the Middle East without fear of being called either anti-Semitic or anti-Arab, we cut our risk of escalating violence.

To argue for balance is not as sexy as being passionate about one side of an issue, but if we're going to live in a civil society, I believe we need to be balanced, open, and tolerant. Fanaticism produces martyrs, not seers.

Love,

Dad

Joe's family includes (from left) his son Sam, to whom the letters in this book are addressed; adopted daughter Riza; Joe; his wife, Rosario Escañan (with canine companion Benaue on her lap); and adopted sons Anthony (rear) and Ricardo.

Photo: Veronica Smith

PPL Industries is a job-training program for disadvantaged people in the core city of Minneapolis. The nonprofit work program has two mottoes: "Creating dignity through work," and "Give me a fish and I eat for a day; teach me to fish and I eat for a lifetime."

Photo: Kerri Jamison

PPL family and housing specialist Libby Welch works with residents such as Marzia and her family.

Joe's ordination class included 21 of its original 30 members plus the Prior and the Student Master. Joe is in the back row, sixth from right. On his left (fifth from right) is classmate Dan Turner, one of this book's contributors.

Photo: Vange Ortega

This young carpenter trainee is a participant in the PPL Youth Build program, which offers job training and leadership development opportunities to high school students through the construction and rehabilitation of affordable housing.

8. Altruism

From the play *Joe*

... the Rich Uncle did come to their house and did come to their parties. I think this says good things about Joe and about his family. About Joe's mother's family as well. Joe's mother's family were quite close. The Rich Dentist sounds like he was not brought up to be a snob. The Dentist gave his sister who lived with them money on regular basis. But you were never supposed to ask a family member for money. "Everyone was very proud to be self sufficient."

And there it is at last! The magic phrase. The touchstone of Joe and PPL. Self Sufficient! The bull's-eye on Joe's famous drawing of a target. They still have his simple drawing at PPL. Really. I saw it—the same drawing that Joe made many, many years ago. Sort of like an archeological artifact. It is a series of concentric circles, each one larger that the next, forming what looks like a target. In the center circle are the letters SS. They stand not for the Nazi organization, but for Self Sufficiency! Next is Job Training and Jobs. This equals personal dignity. The next circle is Housing and means you are putting down roots. And in the outside circle is Neighborhood, which is caring about something outside of yourself—something greater than yourself. Caring about something greater than himself is what Joe has been doing for his entire adult life.

The Phone Call!

by Susan Flagler

As soon as you hear the voice with the slow-paced, slightly nasal tone, you know! As usual, it starts out friendly and low-key, with questions about kids, parents, even pets. You wait for the pitch! In my case "the pitch" was usually on behalf of a currently homeless person who risked death if returned to his/her homeland. Joe knew I had an empty bed; I had no extra money at that point in my life—the early 70s—but I had an empty bed. The next part of the spiel reminded me of my mother getting me to eat my squash by somehow relating my wasting food to the "starving children" in fill-in-the-blank. It went something close to this: "You know, you have more than do 90 percent of the people in the world." Possibly true, but I was raising two children alone on my salary from a non-profit and my imagination. Being in the top 10 percent didn't preclude a little need and a lot of desperation. Joe would continue, "It seems to me it is only just that you give this person refuge."

My favorite of a string of people who lived with us was the woman "...who would be such a help with household chores." Her first question was, "Where do the servants live?" She was the daughter of a deposed governor and had always had servants. So much for help.

What is fascinating about this ability of Joe's is that it stems from a true commitment to help improve the lives of the less fortunate, to provide a path for them to help themselves. His own chosen meager lifestyle (I'm talking about material goods only), left, or rather leaves you with little to argue about, unless you want to appear to be a selfish, materialistic pig!

To complete the above story, our house guest finally was asked to leave. Not because she found my time in a bubble bath a great time to come into the bath, sit by the tub and chat, (no locks on the bathroom door, for kids' safety), not because 20 minutes before I was hosting a baby shower she asked me to iron her blouse. No, the end of my patience came on a weekday morning. I flew down the stairs to get breakfast on the table, kids to school and me to work. I noticed a pair of men's dress shoes in the front hall. Hmmmm! Soon our illustrious house guest comes into the kitchen with a "gentleman," all agiggle. OK—we could have handled this with a talk about house rules, etc. I am thinking this through when the phone rings. A very distraught woman begins to scream at me, calling me everything but nice. You guessed it! She is the wife of the owner of the men's dress shoes. This ended the stay of our elegant house guest.

Joe has touched so many lives, improved the lives of thousands. His many gifts have been used throughout his life to provide for the underprivileged. He truly has followed his passion. All who are fortunate enough to call him friend count themselves lucky, even if at times he's produced aggravation among those drained and made defenseless by his persistence.

Susan Flagler is a past PPL Board Member and past PPL Staff member, as well as a retired executive of Right Management Co. And an active grandma.

Joe Had Plans for Me

by James P. Shannon

On October 1st, 1974 my wife, Ruth, and I moved back to Minnesota after six years in New Mexico. For me it was a welcome homecoming. For Ruth it was a new experience, quite different from life in her hometown, Rochester, New York, and from her years of employment in the U.S. Senate in Washington, D.C.

I was coming home to succeed Russ Ewald as the Executive Director of the Minneapolis Foundation. Ruth had heard, from me and others, many glowing tales about the culture, the marvels, the opportunity, the beauty and the wonderful people of Minnesota. In New Mexico she had been a volunteer at St. Vincent's Hospital in Santa Fe and later at St. Joseph's Hospital in Albuquerque. She was eager to find a new role as a volunteer in Minnesota.

Providentially, one of her first new friends here was Joe Selvaggio. True to his pattern of recruiting new talent, Joe invited Ruth to volunteer on his staff at PPL. She gladly accepted and thoroughly enjoyed being introduced to the dynamic non-profit sector here by her well-connected new boss.

Joe had different plans for me. He wanted us to buy the big rambling house, now PPL headquarters in Minneapolis, at 2516 Chicago Avenue. We begged off, saying that we needed a smaller house. It is difficult to say "No" to Joe, especially to Joe in his chosen role as a "housefinder" for homeless people.

We have always considered ourselves blessed in having Joe as a new friend and guide in our lives at a time when each of us was starting over and finding our way in new careers.

Project for Pride in Living was still in its infancy. Originally started by Joe as a way to find and renovate affordable housing, PPL and Joe quickly learned that their clients needed more than affordable housing. They needed jobs, training, health care, transportation, legal counsel, education and, above all, encouragement. PPL readily and quickly expanded its facilities, its staff, and a whole new range of social services, not to mention a sophisticated and energetic fund-raising arm.

Joe also became part of my support team as I strove to learn the ropes of being a foundation executive. He introduced me to many of his peers in both the grant-seeking and the grant-making sectors of the non-profit world. He had been a protégé of Russ Ewald and had acquired a liberal education in the twin arts of grant-seeking and grant-making. He gladly and generously shared these skills with me.

I had known Joe earlier, when he was a Dominican priest at Holy Rosary parish in Minneapolis and I was a neighboring pastor at Saint Helena's parish in South Minneapolis. That earlier bond made it possible for Joe and me to build a whole new friendship as we strove to harness the good will and the resources of Minneapolis to create level playing fields for many worthy constituencies dedicated to this goal.

Through Joe's passionate dedication to helping the poor and the disenfranchised, he set a new standard for philanthropists and providers of social services in the Twin Cities. He was and is a model for each of us who engages in this worthy and honorable pursuit. Individually, and as a group, we owe a very large debt to Joe's vision, energy, dedication and especially to his basic "theology of service to others".

In helping Joe build his budget for 1976, Ruth was surprised to learn that his salary was only $12,000. She told him that she thought this amount was entirely too modest. (She is not shy). He patiently explained that PPL was created to help the poor. Hence it was prudent for him to keep his salary small. Some days later Ruth and I were having lunch with Russ Ewald, who was then Director of the McKnight Foundation, the largest endowed foundation in Minnesota. Ruth asked Russ whether he thought Joe's projected salary for himself was too small. Russ quickly agreed that it was too modest. Ruth did not know at that time that Joe was in the process of seeking a support grant from McKnight for PPL. Ruth had no further dialog with Joe or Russ about that pending grant, but when McKnight approved the grant, it was approved on condition that Joe's salary would be increased substantially.

All of us working in the non-profit sector at this time realize that in the present economy, the next few years will be extremely difficult for us. As we plan for this future it is comforting to realize that Joe Selvaggio, Steve Cramer and Jim Scheibel have carefully built a competent and dedicated staff at PPL to guide us through this challenging era.

These staff members are committed to the "theology of service to others". As individuals and as a group they understand and endorse the words of Hubert Humphrey when he said that any society would be judged by the way it treats its most fragile and needy members. PPL is dedicated to this high standard of social justice.

As the founding father of PPL Joe Selvaggio deserves great credit for building the solid infrastructure of PPL Through the generosity of the Louis W. Hill, Jr. family and the wisdom of the Humphrey Institute at the University of Minnesota Joe is the recipient this year of an endowed fellowship at the Humphrey Institute. His research and his writing in during this year should give our community and the PPL new insights into the dignity and the meaning of our service to society and new energy to pursue this worthy goal.

James P. Shannon was the founding Chairman of the Minnesota Council on Foundations, and served as its CEO for its first six years. He was the former president of the college of St. Thomas, auxiliary bishop of the diocese of St. Paul-Minneapolis, and executive director of the Minneapolis and General Mills Foundations.

From Joe's letters to Sam:

Dear Sam,

What are the defining issues or influences of your age? The Middle East? Iraq? Global warming? Rock Stars? In my time (I consider the '60s as my time) as a young man, the issues seemed obvious.

This Middle East problem alone makes the '60s look easy. At least when I was your age the moral imperatives were clear—get out of Vietnam, secure civil rights for all minorities, and boycott grapes, an effort I was heavily involved in. As you know, your brother Anthony's middle name is *Cesar*, and your brother Ricardo's middle name is *Chavez*. That's because we got to give them middle names when we adopted them, and we adopted them right at the time I was the Twin Cities organizer for the Grape Boycott, led by Cesar Chavez.

Cesar was big in the '60s and early '70s. When Bobby Kennedy was alive he went out to visit Cesar and left a bunch of young organizers behind to help Cesar in his fight with the growers. It was all part of the "war on poverty" atmosphere, although the formal "War on Poverty" didn't come into being until President Johnson gave it a label.

The growers of lettuce and grapes were paying their workers—mostly Mexican-Americans—a mere pittance, and gave them shacks to live in. These organizers, with the Kennedy name behind them, brought the issue of the exploited "migrant workers" to all Americans. Since the farm workers couldn't make a great deal of progress as a start-up union fighting against some powerful growers, they organized a boycott of the products. First it was lettuce, and then grapes.

Grape-pickers were sent out to all the major cities in the U.S. and asked to organize picket lines in front of the supermarkets and to try to get the owners not to buy the California grapes. The picker they sent to the Twin Cities was Pete Cardenas. He came with a wife, two beautiful children, and a beat-up Chevy. Somehow he got in touch with me and asked for my help.

Since I had just quit my 10-day old job at Honeywell because I found out I was making containers for anti-personnel bombs (I'll tell you more about that when I write about the arc of my life), I was interested in helping—even making a job out of it. Cardenas was interested in having me help because he knew how to pick grapes, but knew nothing about organizing a boycott in a cold Minnesota city. He said his office would be willing to pay me $50 a week—which sounded like a lot to him, because he was only getting $5 per week plus modest expenses. But there was a small catch. *I* had to raise the $50 per week locally. What a deal!

What the hell. I had contacts. It was a good cause that was in the news. I thought I shouldn't have any trouble raising the $50 per week for my salary. We shook on it and I was hired. Things were simple in those days.

But I quickly found out that I loved the job but hated the work. It was a noble job—working for exploited minority farm-workers. The Churches supported the boycott, and my heroes MLK and RFK were behind the cause. But the work was tough. I had to call up friends and ask them to join me on the picket line. Besides asking them to give up their time and a bit of money, I had to expose them to some hostile shoppers.

A typical Saturday afternoon would consist of meeting at a Red Owl supermarket with a bunch of ratty-looking homemade signs, braving the rain or the snow, and asking the shoppers coming into the store to shop elsewhere—or at least to not buy grapes. The typical response was, "But this is my store. I have a great deal of loyalty to this neighborhood store. I promise I won't buy grapes." But sometimes you'd get an atypical response and the shopper would yell, "Get a job! Mind your own business!"

I realized that I did not like being the object of scorn—especially for only $50 per week. I suffered through six months of that grueling work without seeing much in the way of results. It was a good cause, but the psychic reward I was getting from knowing I was on the side of the angels was not as great as the psychic pain I was receiving from being rebuffed and seeing no results. It was tough to turn in my resignation to Cardenas, but I had to do it.

A couple of months later I went to a talk at the University of St. Thomas by Saul Alinsky, the great community organizer from Chicago. During the Q and A I asked Saul about his theory of organizing people out of their "self-interest." I said, "Not all organizing has to be done out of self-interest—look at the Grape Boycott."

He said, "It won't last. There's not enough self-interest." He was right. It didn't last, and we didn't get results.

But one other time, Alinsky was wrong. He held a three-day workshop with organizers from all over the country. At the wind-up session, when he had about 400 people in the gym, he said to them, "And if you go back to your respective cities and you apply what you learned here to your local situations, you'll not only be the best goddamn organizer in your city, but it will put two inches on your dick."

Then my friend Ellen Pence rose from her chair and asked, "Now Saul, what am I going to do with a two-inch dick?"

Love ya,

Dad

P.S. This is really what existentialism is all about—taking a stand or being screwed by the stands taken by someone else.

Thucydides said, "Unless we who are not injured are as indignant as those who are, justice will never come." On the other hand, a Don Quixote I am not. I like results too much. So much for the romance of activism.

9. Mind, Body and Spirit

The Opposite of Self-Centeredness

by Terry Thompson

Joe has a gift for friendship. If you could pick at birth one of the gifts you would like generously bestowed, and that would stay with you for a lifetime, this is something you might choose. It would compete with good health on a cosmic list of blessings, and it's this gift for friendship that has helped make Joe a good man. There's a local newspaper columnist who has a reputation for calling nearly everyone a "close, personal friend." He usually means people in high places, but the predictability of the remark and the fact that it's such an exaggeration have made the boast something of a joke. Nobody could be that close to so many people, and it's clear that when the expression's used, it's meant to flatter the person who makes the claim.

That's not the case with Joe. I don't hear him dropping names in search of compliments or admiration. When he mentions some prominent politician or a rich benefactor, it's always in context. He never needs to prove his worth by reminding you of how many people like him. He remembers easily and with empathy the names of countless poor people. He'd be disappointed in himself if he forgot any of them.

This is the opposite of self-centeredness, not that Joe lacks for self-esteem. People want to say they are friends of Joe. This probably goes back to the early hardscrabble days when Joe needed a way to support himself. He started by asking people if they would underwrite his work in the inner city with a small donation. Get enough people and you've got a living wage, which is exactly the way it worked out. Guilt was a factor in this beneficence. If you were a comfortable suburbanite, for example, with a gnawing conscience about what you were not doing to help the underserved, investing in Joe and letting him do good works by proxy was a satisfactory arrangement for both parties. It was clean and not personally disruptive. The giver felt better for this act of charity, and Joe marched more confidently on his neighborhood rounds, while strengthening ties with people who would be invaluable later on in powering PPL and related causes.

Most of these people were sincere about their relationships with Joe, though some just used him for what I call the "virtue by association" factor. Over time, a group of friends materialized who were conscientious and willing to spend money and energy abetting Joe's efforts. There were others who tagged along just because it was cool to say they were friends of Joe Selvaggio, someone toughing it out and making a name in the community. True friends outnumber the other kind. The phonies say nice things to his face but behind his back make fun of his irritating traits, including his stubbornness, his pronounced frugality, and a sense of himself that can get puffed up after too much attention. Some close friends may poke fun at some of Joe's traits, but they do so to his face, with great affection. I hope Joe can spot the difference. Either way, he never stops making friends; and he never stops meeting people who want to make friends with him. It's a gift, of which I have been a recipient on many occasions.

One prolonged episode stands out in my memory. Retiring from a job and a corporation after a decade of Sisyphean struggle, and writing for deadline a graduate school thesis on the side, I was feeling close to mental paralysis. Burned out and brain dead. The stronger the hold on me, the angrier and more introspective I became.

I needed company, but I shut out all friends, and that's where Joe came in. Sensing my difficulty in the most human terms, he telephoned 12 consecutive nights, each time with a different idea that might help me to heal. In return he got indifference and occasional insults, because in my predicament I could not think of a single reason our friendship should be preserved. The more I pushed him away, the more he seemed determined to reach out. Eventually this concentrated display of persistence and concern helped me climb out of a dark hole. The day I finally gave in to his relentlessness, to his decency, and surfaced at last in the world, we went to one of those ridiculous "jiggle" movies that we knew our wives would never see. Afterward, we analyzed the movie and laughed at its silliness, and that night I slept soundly for the first time in months. The next day Joe called again, acting like nothing out of the ordinary had happened, and offered a new idea to keep me out of my funk and keep my spirits rising. Soon we were off on another small adventure, he at the wheel of that big hand-me-down car, I on the passenger side smiling, a couple of friends just driving around.

Terry Thompson is the former head of Public Relations for the Pillsbury Corp., a writer, and adjunct Professor at the University of St. Thomas.

From Joe's letters to Sam

Dear Sam,

What do the late U.S. Senator Paul Wellstone, ad executive Lee Lynch, and gramma (my mother) have in common? I'd say they are or were three of the happiest people I've known. Each was a pleasure to be around. Each seemed happy for different reasons. All were genetically happy (about 50% of the game), but they also cultivated happiness through their *mind, body, and spirit.*

First, let's think about Paul Wellstone. I don't know if you ever met Paul, but you certainly know him from his fiery speeches on T.V. Paul was not a particularly handsome man. In fact, he's been called "funny looking"—kind of Harpo Marx looking. His politics were way to the left of the average American. He stood 5'6" tall and walked with a severe limp—hardly star qualities.

He was the poorest member of the Senate, and his professor's salary before he entered the Senate didn't give him a chance to acquire any capital.

His body was racked with pain from multiple sclerosis and a back injury he incurred during his college wrestling days. But the "ghost in the machine" wouldn't be stifled by his body. With all the bodily or physical disadvantages, Paul still rose to great heights as a Senator. Even though he kept his body in reasonable shape through weight lifting and stretch exercises, his strength for happiness came from his spirit and his mind. You never met him without feeling inspired by his engagement with an issue. He'd be jumping up and down on the campaign trail yelling, "We're gonna win! We're gonna win!" or he'd be pounding the lectern on behalf of the needy urging us to fight the polluters of our environment.

His happiness came from being caught up in the fray. He was not self absorbed, but absorbed by the challenges of getting a better life for all. His generous spirit saved him from self-indulgent unhappiness.

Lee Lynch, on the other hand, is a different kind of guy—just as happy, but not particularly altruistic. His genes bring him 90% of his happiness. I suspect he'd still be called "Glee Lynch" even if he were in politics or manual labor rather than in business.

Lee walks around asking questions like, "Are you getting enough?" or "what's giving you heartburn today?" always expecting to entice an upbeat smile or creative comment from you.

Lee's spirit or soul genuinely likes other people. He's interested in learning about them—especially if they are different from him—old, black, female, young, foreign, or weird looking. People don't bore him. Even if people are boring, he tries to figure out what makes them boring and consequently stays interested in their story.

Lee eats too much, and he generously feeds you too much when you visit his home. But he does exercise and constantly extols the benefits of a well-tuned body and a clear-thinking mind. He made a brilliant career in advertising and devoted time and treasure to reviving the downtown district of Minneapolis. He creative juices flow like his adored Mississippi. Leland is a true Irish elf. Yet, even though he's been dubbed "Glee" Lynch by some folks, he has a razor-sharp business mind, as Jim Binger noted.

The third happy person, my mother, seemed happy because of different attributes. She, like Wellstone and Lynch was not self-absorbed, but she was very much into her own family. She had a large family so she didn't need a great number of friends. Looking out for the welfare of family members was enough to keep her busy. A day never went by without her calling a sister or son and asking how their children were doing. "Was the job O.K.? Is the pay enough? Is the school good?"

She liked a nice house. Aunt Bess told me once, "Your mother likes nice things." She said it in a way that told me she was somewhat surprised, because my mother was such a spiritual person. And spiritual people shouldn't "like nice things."

While it was true that she wanted quality furniture and decent jewelry, she never overspent, and didn't really covet them. She let material comforts serve her and her family, but her *spirituality*, her *attitude*, were the forces that kept her grounded in happiness.

She didn't exercise much, but she ate carefully. She knew that if she didn't keep her body healthy she couldn't do any of the other things she wanted to do.

So, three very different people attaining happiness in three distinct combinations of body, mind, and spirit—all working well off their "core competencies."

What are your core competencies? How well are your physical, mental and spiritual lives integrated? You seem to be happy despite the fact that you haven't acquired any wealth, your body doesn't give you "hunk" stature, and you've never been at the top 10% of your class. I'm not saying you're "disadvantaged," but I also wouldn't put you in the "specially gifted" category. I think you (and I) are fortunate to have been born with a pretty well-integrated mind/body/spirit relationship. And we haven't blown it—yet.

Love,

Dad

• • •

Dear Sam:

Some more thoughts on mind, body, spirit. Two people who enhanced my perception of mind, body, and spirit are Jayme Sussner and Ming Whatever. (Ming doesn't use a last name). Jayme is my physical trainer. Ming is a Chinese medical doctor who refused to sit for the U.S.'s M.D degree because he prefers the Chinese system of seeking wellness.

First, Jayme, a handsome former college football player with a master's degree in the science of physical performance. Jayme became my trainer about three years ago when I decided to invest some time and money in my body so it would last longer. Once or twice a week I subject myself to the unreasonable demands of Jayme with the unfounded belief that if I follow his instructions I'll end up stronger, more flexible, and pain-free well into the future. So far my only consolation is the belief that if I do *not* go to Jayme, the aging process will make me weaker, stiffer, and pain-filled.

When I put myself in Jayme's hands—usually about 2:00 p.m. on a weekday afternoon, he greets me with "let's go, let's go, let's go!" I respond with, "Slow down; let's go easy today. Be merciful."

He is unmoved. He cranks up the treadmill until I'm in a jog. I plead, "Five minutes?"

"Ten minutes—no whining or we do 12," he responds with disdain. I keep my mouth shut because he means it.

After the 10 minutes, with salty sweat burning into my eyes, he hustles me over to the lateral pull bar. He sets it at 10—I suggest a somewhat easier 12. He says with contempt, "12 and we do two sets." I submit to 10.

This goes on for about 15 more exercises on different machines for 30 *long* minutes.

At the end I'm whipped. He says, "Coming in Thursday?"

I say, "No way. My muscles, tendons, and ligaments need at least a week to heal."

With a grimace he yells, "Wimp! See you next week. Don't be late."

And to think I'm paying him big bucks to treat me like this—me a 66-year-old seasoned man—he, a twenty something guy who got hit upside the helmet too many times. But I go back, each week, because my muscles do benefit. My balance is better, and it even clears my mind.

Ming, now, is the polar opposite of Jayme. Jayme's a hunk. Ming, while healthy looking, is a bit on the skinny side. He's the ascetic Buddhist monk, formerly a doctor of Chinese medicine.

Ming greets me with sage words like, "remember, it's 90% mental." Or, "When I meditate I try to think of nothing." Or "The body needs to be relaxed for energy to flow."

I first met Ming when he was practicing Chinese medicine on the west bank of the University of Minnesota. He had an office in a small home just off Cedar and Washington Avenues. His office reminded me of Dr. Pelettieri's office on the West side of Chicago—the office I visited as a child 50 some years ago.

On the first visit Ming was trying to get rid of some of my neck pain. I lay prone with my face in the hole of his massage table. After about 10 minutes of manipulation on my back and neck, I felt the pressure change slightly. "Is he walking on my back?" I thought. At the end of the treatment I mentioned something about the "back-walk" and he said, "What back-walk?" with a mysterious grin on his face. Apparently he took pride in trying to walk on patient's backs without them noticing the shift from hand manipulation to feet manipulation. He constantly has that mystical angelic "soul quality" to him.

The second time I saw Ming he was out in some small town in Wisconsin, population, 890. He lived in a decrepit farmhouse near some wavy hills. I said to him, "Ming, what are you doing out here"?

He answered, "I don't know why my master sent me here. He said this is holy ground. See those hills? They look like a dragon, don't they? My Master thought the spirits were good here."

I remember thinking, "This guy is too mystical for me. Masters telling him to do something and he does it? Holy grounds? Much too superstitious for me! I like science. I like logic."

Yet there is something good about Ming's spirit that is good for *my* spirit. He has stayed healthy, not by doing 15 reps on 35 pound dumbbells like Jayme, but by remaining at peace with his environment. He meditates long, has few friends, and eats vegetables. But he is strong and happy.

I appreciate both Jayme and Ming. I do my reps in a scientific way to strengthen my muscles. Then I try to "think of nothing." I try to be more intuitive, more in awe of the mysterious wonders of the world, more imaginative. The world is, after all, made up of the physical—things we can touch and expand, like muscles. Still, the non-physical world, (the mind and the spirit) can do wonders to the body, just by thinking. Imagine the lemon taste and experience your saliva changing. Imagine the joy simple images give us.

Maybe our bodily and spiritual health *is* 90 percent mental. Our task is to remain open.

Night,

Dad

10. Right to Left to Center: a Political Journey

From the play *Joe*

… Joe got caught in the ’60s. The Kennedys, Jack and Bobby. Martin Luther King, Jr. The Vietnam War. But not the drug culture. He was a part of the Protest Movement. When Joe was a priest he turned in his draft card even though, as a priest, he could not be drafted. So Joe was continuing to float through his life when he got caught by the changes around him. Much the same as I did. Much the same as millions of people of our generation. People like Joe and I who had something burning way down deep but were just going along not knowing how to figure out how to get at that fire inside of us. Then the world started to change around us. Everything we had been taught was solid as the earth began to change. So for people like Joe and I the earth literally began to move and shift out from under our feet. And for both of us it was the beginning of the awakening to ourselves.

I found the theater and the reason for my life. Joe found his stride in working for the poor. Joe’s world began to shake and quake. He was faced with his whole world changing. He no longer agreed with his family or his older brother or his friends about the state of the world. Joe was a Democrat, and his family and friends were all Republicans. All the guys he grew up with were Republicans. They disagreed about John Kennedy. They disagreed about the Vietnam War. They disagreed about Civil Rights and Martin Luther King and civil disobedience, breaking the law. Joe and all of them disagreed about all that. Joe disagreed with his Church [about] the White Church and Black Church in Louisiana. He was having trouble with the whole no-sex thing, celibacy. So Joe was having trouble and doubts about his Church. And to be honest, his Church was having serious doubts about Joe as well. Joe was accused of caring more for the outside part more than the inside part, caring more about them than about us. In fact, the Church, like his mother, had the feeling that maybe Joe wasn’t cut out for the life of a priest.

• • •

[Joe and I] were talking about the shooting of John Kennedy. We agreed that Lyndon Johnson did great things on Civil Rights but was tragically wrong on Vietnam. It’s my belief that Lyndon couldn’t pull out of Vietnam because he was from Texas, and his Texasness made it impossible for Lyndon to think of quitting in Vietnam. That just goes against the Laws of The Cowboy Commandments. Joe grew up with his Commandments, but so did I—and so it seems did Lyndon. I was taught under the Cowboy Commandments that you “Never Back Down; Never Apologize; Never Give Up; and Prefer Death Before Dishonor!” Poor Lyndon was caught in his past and who that made him. Man, I know the feeling.

Then Joe said that of all people it was Richard Nixon who got us out of Vietnam. In a disgraceful manner but out. The photograph of the last U.S. helicopter taking off from the roof of the American Embassy in Saigon is something every young American boy should study, as well as the leader of every nation thinking about going to war on our side. If there is one thing worse than being America's enemy it is being Americas friend. Ask a lot of Mexican people. They have a saying in Mexico. "Poor Mexico. So far from God; so close to the United States." Joe said that Nixon had opened China and, while it was for all the wrong reasons, he did get us out of Vietnam. He did do some good things. He started the EPA I said. But he couldn't make it in the Republican Party today. Nixon is much, much too far to the left to make it in the Republican Party today. Joe said, "I know. It's weird." I said, "Richard Nixon is also not nearly mean enough for these guys today."

I asked Joe if he got to choose where the Church sent him or did they just send him where they wanted. "Pretty much the latter," he said. "There was a little more independence when I came in. So I got to ask for an area. I said I wanted to serve the poor. Because I'm really excited by the whole War On Poverty and the Secular Saint idea. The Church improving this world because the kingdom of God is within and we have to improve this world to make it heavenly as much as possible." That sounds good to me. To make the world heavenly! What a fantastic goal!

The Internship in Chicago. What did he think when he stepped out the door and there was not a White face. Little Joe who grew up without ever having a Black friend... in Grade School, High School and three years of college you meet maybe two Black people. No Black people in your life and now when you open the door there is nothing but Black people. How did that feel? "Good," he said.

• • •

Being a priest meant Mother Church sent little Joe Selvaggio, who was the apple of his biological mother's eye, who was used to being able to skate and coast through life, to someplace in a slum where he and the few other Church workers were the only white faces. Or then Mother Church send him into the heart of Redneck America, a small town in the swamps of Louisiana! Joe began to see the world in a different way because he was seeing a different world.

From Joe's letters to Sam

Dear Sam,

As you know, I've spent most of my life helping the poor get a better life. I've been very fortunate to have had enough rich friends support me so I could "make a living" helping the poor. Lots of folks volunteer to help the poor. I did it for a living! "Is this a great country, or what?"

The start of this journey was in the seminary—when I was a conservative. I had just finished reading Barry Goldwater's book, *Conscience of a Conservative*. My brother John was promoting the book. As kids we didn't use the terms *liberal* and *conservative*.

We were from a hard working immigrant family so we really didn't identify with the poor. (All Americans basically think of themselves as middle class.) We gave a little money to the missions in Africa, but Africans were poor because they were stuck in Africa. We assumed that the poor in America were poor because they were too lazy to work hard and make more money. Senator Goldwater made his case against welfare as an "enabling" instrument, and I bought it.

I remember trying to advocate that position to another seminarian, a Mike Duffy, and he actually got mad at me. He said I couldn't be a good Catholic, let alone a priest, if I held to those Fascist ideas. Hadn't I read the Papal Encyclicals about wealth sharing and social responsibilities? I was so new to the field and he said it with such conviction, that I assumed he was right.

Mike's preaching at me made me pay much closer attention to what Martin Luther King, Jr. (MLK) was saying. And MLK put a human face on poverty and put it into a religious context. Now "helping the poor" became participating in the mission of Jesus. And that's what, after all, I had chosen to do as a priest.

When the *March on Selma* was in the news, I think every seminarian in the country wanted to run down to Selma, Alabama to help get the Blacks their voting and "riding-in-the-front-of-the-bus" rights. Bishop James P. Shannon of Minneapolis was there, but our superiors said our job, now, was to study and prepare for the struggle.

When I was assigned to Holy Rosary parish in 1966, I was given the opportunity to not just be a parish priest, but to be an advocate for the poor in their fight for a better life. I got into the homes of our low-income parishioners and wanted something better for them. Whether they were black, white, or American Indian, they all wanted better living conditions, more income, and a better chance for their children.

One family in particular, I grew close to—that of Alice McHie, a single parent, black woman in her mid-forties. She had 5 children: Ronnie, Frances, James, Michael, and David. Ten other children of hers died during childbirth. Alice worked in a hot commercial laundry operation in the north side of Minneapolis. Once I visited her on the job. I had never before experienced such working conditions. It must have be 110 degrees in there with 90 percent humidity. I had to get out in less than two minutes. I couldn't understand how the workers could stay in that atmosphere for 8 hours. I remember thinking "Those damn conservatives. They have the nerve to call poor people lazy. I'd like to see how long they could last working in those conditions. I'll bet the owner is sitting in an air-conditioned office figuring out how to get an anti-union Republican politician elected so he could make more money and keep wages low."

My respect for Alice grew because of her job. But it grew even more when I saw the difficulty Alice had in dealing with her children. The kids all had rather charming personalities, but they didn't have the strong work ethic that Alice had, and Alice didn't have the time to be with them much, the way my mother was with us. Alice was off in that ultra hot laundry shop and the kids all ended up having some brushes with the law. I started to see the value of both welfare to help single parents have time to parent, and birth control to keep the number of children down to a manageable level. My conservative upbringing began to get tempered by the need for some liberal solutions like welfare and birth control.

After I left the priesthood, partly because the Church wasn't moving fast enough on solutions like birth control, I met a businessman, Ted Pouliot. Ted urged me to start Project for Pride in Living. Ted said to me, "We could have the motto 'Give me a fish and I'll eat for a day. Teach me to fish and I'll eat for a lifetime.' Without the poor helping themselves, we don't stand a chance to help them. And besides, it will be a lot easier to raise money from conservative business people if they know the poor are pulling their weight—just getting a hand up, not a hand out."

My conservative principles came back into play. I remember thinking, "Am I playing into the hands of the conservative who think the poor are lazy if we take the "teaching to fish" phrase as our motto?" After some thought I said, no, it's a good principle. The poor do need to work hard like Alice McHie. If we expose people like Alice to conservatives they'll realize that there is a limit to how hard people can work. They'll bend and liberals will bend, reaching a great partnership. I think PPL has used the best of both worlds without giving in to the worst in each position.

Now I call myself both liberal and conservative. I think Mike Duffy was right. I'm proud to be a centrist. I'm very comfortable to have moved from right to left to center.

Love,

Dad

• • •

Dear Sam:

In the early spring of 2003 I got a call. The dialogue went something like this.

"Hi, is this Joe Selvaggio?"

"Yes."

"This is Camille Gage. I'm calling for the new Dean of the Humphrey Institute, Brian Atwood. Brian would like to set up a meeting to pick your brain on philanthropy."

"Sure, how about some afternoon at PPL, say around 3:00 or 4:00 p.m. any day in the next month?"

"Well, the Dean is very busy. He'd like you to come to him here at the Humphrey."

I immediately thought of a story I had heard about Jim Shannon, President of the General Mills Foundation, and the then-Mayor of Minneapolis, Don Fraser. Fraser had made an appointment and when they met up in Shannon's office in Golden Valley, Shannon greeted Fraser with, "Mr. Mayor, you didn't have to come out here to see me. You're a busy man, I'd have come to you."

To which Fraser responded, "Thank you, but I'm the one asking for something here. It's more fitting that I come to you."

Shannon, one of the truly humble men of our time, who'd given up a bishopric and the presidency of a major college over issues of principle, was a towering example for all of us.

I thought, "The Dean is the one asking for something. It's more fitting that he should come to me." But I bit my tongue and said, "Sure, what's a good time?"

A few days later, when I arrived at Dean Atwood's office, he said to me, "Well, we'd like to give you an Award. And it's not just an honor and a plaque. This award comes with a $100,000 stipend."

"You're kidding," I said. Praise the Lord Jesus that I hadn't given in to pride and said on the phone, "If the Dean wants to see me, he can come to me." I could have blown $100,000!

The Dean continued, "I'm not kidding. You've been selected by an anonymous panel of judges to receive the first Louis W. Hill, Jr. Award to be administered by the Humphrey Institute. The Hill family gave the money through its family foundations, the Northwest Area Foundation and the Grotto Foundation."

Damn, did he say the Northwest Area Foundation? This time I thought I really should fall off my chair. About two weeks earlier I had received a call from a reporter from *City Pages,* the local alternative newspaper for the Twin Cities. As a favor to a friend, Arthur Himmelman, I had agreed to talk to the reporter even though I knew the article would not be favorable. I'd reasoned, now that I've been out of PPL for 5 years, I can be more open, less guarded in my opinions without having my associates feel the consequences if I offend someone. If those of us who are "retired" can't say what's on our minds, then who?

As I sat before the Dean I remembered that I had been careful with the reporter—I had told him I had no facts—just impressions. I had cited some good things about the foundation (their courage to try something new, their focus on eliminating a pocket of poverty), but I also remembered that *City Pages* is known for its aggressive journalism. Most likely they would ignore the positive points and emphasize the negatives.

Lordy, lordy, I had done it again. Bit the hand the feeds me—this time to the tune of $100,000. It had taken me a lifetime to save $100,000 for my retirement. Now I got (or almost got) another $100,000—a perfect amount for me to put into my retirement fund, giving me enough money to live off of and never have to work for money again.

Would they withdraw the award if the article comes out tomorrow? Will they be embarrassed? Will I be embarrassed? Should I try to get something in writing so they won't withdraw the award? Should I tell the dean? Should I call the reporter?

The questions were racing through my mind. I thought of John Mitchell saying that Katherine Graham of the Washington Post "got her tit caught in the wringer this time." (Only, his subject being Watergate, it was his tit that was caught.)

I decided to keep quiet—to tell only a few trusted friends. I was confident that if the reporter heard about the award he'd probably put my picture in the paper and make a big deal out of it. Prayer was out of the question. Even if God does intervene in our worldly affairs, he/she certainly wouldn't stoop to get me $100,000.

I sweated over this looming problem for about 6 weeks. Every Wednesday I'd check the new edition of *City Pages* and be relieved when I didn't see the story on the cover. "Maybe they killed the story because they couldn't get enough dirt," I thought. Wouldn't that be nice?

Then one evening at the movies I ran into a couple of old friends, Marci Shapiro and Dick Mammond. They congratulated me for "telling the truth" about the NW Area Foundation in *City Pages*."

"My God," I said, "Is it out? I haven't seen it."

I rushed to the nearby drugstore to pick up a copy even before sitting down for the movie. Sure enough, my quote suggesting the need for some watchdog organization to monitor NWAF's spending cuts was there—not just in the story's text, but also displayed in bold capital letters.

Damn. Burned another bridge. A friend reassured me. My quote wasn't that bad. And after all, TIME magazine gave their Person of the Year award to three whistle-blowers last year. Watchdogs are in. They can't be that mad at you.

I never did find out just how mad they were at me, since no one said anything to me. Then, after I sent a conciliatory e-mail and voice mail to the executive director of the foundation, he responded with a gracious e-mail. Whew!

It's hard to tell the truth without burning bridges unnecessarily. There's a difference between "Minnesota Nice" and the dictates of reason. Russ Ewald, the McKnight Foundation's Executive director and a feisty spirit—now sadly departed—was my model. But I also understand that people have their reputations to guard—that their good name is important to their ability to do good work in the community. They have a right to be angry if someone says something negative in the press about them—especially when they don't have the opportunity to respond.

In this instance I think we all squeaked by. And when you put this problem next to issues like the Middle East or North Korean controversies you wonder why I was so worried.

Love,

Dad

11. In the Streets and in the Suites

From the play *Joe*

The Missile Sites. Around 1972. Protest against the atomic missile sights. Joe was at one of the colleges around Fargo-Moorhead at a teach-in. He and a bunch of students and a few teachers bused out to a missile site. They started walking towards the missile site when all of a sudden there were a lot of National Guardsmen. This place was in the middle of nowhere and there was no press there to see what might happen. This was right after Kent State. For a moment Joe was afraid they were going to do the same thing to his group that they had done to protesters at Kent State. Joe remembers this moment as the one time he was really physically afraid.

"I protested every week when I worked for the Grape Boycott and Cesar Chavez. Every damn Saturday I was in front of grocery stores passing out leaflets about the grape boycott. Saul Alinsky said it's about self-interest." Joe said he asked Alinsky about the grape boycott where he is out there freezing his buns off and he doesn't get anything out of it but feeling good for helping farm workers in California. Saul said it would never last. There was not enough self-interest in it for Joe for it to last. "But I think there is often more than self-interest involved," Joe said.

"Once I started Advocate Services and PPL I had to put a stop to all that. I just didn't have the time anymore. And I was starting to get money to do things. Make things happen." A priest friend told the story about the guy who owned a mule, and every time the guy wanted the mule's attention he had to smack it in the head with a board. The priest friend said to Joe that he had been smacking us in the head for a long time and now it was time for Joe to do something. So Joe said to me, "I decided it was time to switch from smacking people in the head to getting something done. But maybe I'll go back. Next year I can start collecting Social Security and I won't have to work, so I wouldn't mind starting protesting again. I wouldn't mind getting arrested again. I wouldn't mind spending some time in jail. I mean, I think I can write in there."

• • •

Here is a part of the Joe magic that makes a lot of us uncomfortable. The PPL has this factory. It puts practically impossible-to-place people in a job. It helps these people, society's outcasts, to get an education and work towards self-sufficiency and self-respect. The factory uses society's garbage, such as the thrown-away TV sets, to put the people to work. PPL takes society's throwaway stuff and castoff people and helps the people make something positive out of what looks like a mess. And the factory makes a little money. How can that be? A left-wing do-gooder action actually makes money?! For ages the Left Wing has believed with almost religious fervor that people doing that kind of thing must lose money! But Joe and PPL set up this business so that it doesn't lose money. Usually. They have had some losers.

But if that happens, they just close that business down and move on. The remark about Joe being an entrepreneur is right on and helps to explain the sprit of PPL. The people who work there are risk-takers. There are people who work at PPL who would tell you that every day at PPL involves some kind of gamble.

• • •

Charismatic leaders like Joe need a lot of very practical, effective people around them. Without the ability to attract such people, Joe would end up being a useless eccentric, spinning his wheels faster and faster while traveling in smaller and smaller circles. But Joe is able to attract extraordinary people to the mission of PPL. From day one, though, it was Joe's show, as we say in show biz. Every day many people did many vital jobs, and if they hadn't done them PPL would have seriously struggled. Without Joe there would have been no PPL in the early days. Joe has always needed a lot of very understanding and dedicated people around him. Together they created a unique and fundamentally important place for people in the city of Minneapolis to come for help, for a helping hand up.

• • •

This was young Joe's Sunday. Playing [a game] with his older brother—and not just any game, but Monopoly! Was Joe good at Monopoly? Somehow I think he was. This is the part of him that was a property wheeler-dealer even at that age.

Joe Selvaggio: Notorious Suspect

by F. X. Kroncke

Joe Selvaggio—a notorious suspect. It's an uneasy truth, both about him and for those who join him in his various projects and campaigns. Joe is a bridge person. He not only points you towards places you more than likely never wanted to go and are still, at this moment, hesitant to approach, but he also takes you there. In person. And as you place your trust in him, your deepest suspicions are aroused.

"Why is he doing this?" everyone asks. It is asked by those he is ostensibly helping. It is asked by those he is ostensibly encouraging to join him in extending their help and wealth. Look at this Joe. *In the streets:* Joe lives in the Phillips Neighborhood of Minneapolis, where he launched Project for Pride in Living (PPL). A former priest, educated, with access to financial means—"Why is he living next door to us? We who live here only because we have no other choice! What's he after?" *Suspicious. In the suites:* "Father Joe—you don't mind if I still call you 'Father' do you? Why not take a job with us? You can do more good as a leader of society. Look at yourself—a learned man, a cut above. Why waste your talents and endanger your life by living there? Come here, we appreciate your skills." *Suspicious. Very suspicious.*

It gets worse. You bought the fact that he can bring money into the neighborhood. You see the homes get rebuilt. You see the pride of ownership. You see the impact of this guy, who you now feel is a friend. You laugh with him. Eat with him. Share his worries. But then he doesn't act like you thought he would and sometimes wished he would. He's not running for political office. He's not taking a raise. You know he deserves it. PPL grows each year. It will reach $13 million in revenues. "Hey, what's with Joe? He should take the dough." He makes you nervous. Takes a pittance for a salary and no pension—not for him or anybody else on the PPL payroll. *Suspect, again.*

It gets worse—in jarring ways. "You see, Joe didn't just ask me for money. He didn't just want funds for PPL, hell, that's the easy part. Watch out for this guy—I mean, I love him, but ... see, he wants me to become part of PPL. No, not just on a committee, but in my life. See, now here's why I'm here tonight, pitching for him... what will happen is, well, he understands that we need to fix up our neighborhood. Go on, laugh. We're rich. Rich and richer. But he wants you and me to be rich, even richer. Hell, he's more comfortable with my being wealthy than I am. Sure, he makes you give—the guy was a Dominican preacher for God's sake!—but he truly wants you to understand what's Good for you, not just get you doing Good." *This guy got some nuts loose? Truly suspicious.*

That's Joe Selvaggio. All the people around him are suspicious. Because he keeps going off into unexpected areas. He's a sixties-bred radical, so you await the diatribe against Corporate America, and a moralistic, hellfire-and-brimstone prophetic denunciation of being rich. "For it is harder for the rich man to get to heaven than it is for a camel to pass through the eye of a needle." Hah! Not from Joe. Sure, he knows Scripture. And, okay, at times, you get Catholic Guilt thrown at you, or the chastisements of Jesus...but that's not all. No, Joe is the same with the poor and the rich. With people in any category or definition, because Joe is interested in relationships.

Actually, it's more fierce than that. Joe is a neighborhood builder. Maybe he didn't sit down and do the philosophy on this before he began, but his slogan emerges: "It takes a neighborhood to build a family." Long before Hillary spoke her own truth, Joe was there, telling everyone—this is Joe, so catch this word, "everyone"—that they are neighbors. And as neighbors that they need each other. Because each one needs to learn how to live with pride and dignity. It's no fluke that it is Project for Pride in Living, because you come to grasp that it is not just the acquisition of wealth in home ownership which renders Pride, but it is the proper use of wealth which renders one dignified. Joe enables the giver and the receiver to grow proud and to bestow dignity each upon the other.

Sound schmaltzy? Hah. You'd have to have been there through the years, the decades. The guy's driven. Relentless. Impoverished. Struggling. Rejected—and rejected again. But he has his own suspicions—about you and me, about us: givers and receivers.

He's still living in Phillips, and there are always those who are still waiting for him to show his true colors. For Joe to expose what he's "really up to." The suspicion never wanes. Now, members of the elite Minneapolis Club have drawn him into their fellowship. He goes there because he sincerely likes these folks. The Club's just another part of Joe's neighborhood. He's no snob. Yet, as he swims and sweats among those blessed with wealth to bestow, so are their suspicions not allayed. "What's this *One Percent Club* really all about? Giving one-percent of our net worth. What's he up to now?"

For some, Joe never seems to go away. And they're right. He's not retiring. He's regrouping. Throughout Minnesota, his latest project still arouses suspicion. He's still the notorious "Joe." *Suspect.* And yet, despite the native caution of the wealthy, they love him.

His latest foray. Cuba. That old stalking horse for both Left and Right. Joe preaches a sermon and praises Castro for his best achievements—literacy, no homeless—and condemns him for his repressive acts. So how, to take him? Hear him? He's preaching at the church he attends, which claims, "We welcome you wherever you are on your journey." Just like Joe, a Big "C" Catholic.

If you want to receive something from Joe's life, simply find a way to become suspicious. Know that when others—both those who give and those who receive—wonder what the hell you're up to, well, then, like Joe, you're onto something. Follow in that pathway. I suspect you'll find your dignity and a pride in living.

Francis Xavier Kroncke is a writer, consultant, and friend of Joe now living in California.

The Most Impolitic Character I Know

By Richard McFarland

I have known Joe Selvaggio for many years, and our relationship has always been exciting and challenging—to say the least. When I think of Joe, I am reminded of the story of a gentleman who was asked at the celebration of his 50th wedding anniversary whether he had ever over those 50 years considered divorce. His reply: "Divorce—no; murder—yes."

Joe can drive me nuts. He is the most impolitic character I know, and I have suggested to him on more than one occasion that he has a tendency to talk when he should be listening. He can say the dumbest things at exactly the wrong time. His off-the-cuff comments have caused me more problems than anyone else I know. He knew perfectly well that I was a Trustee of the Minneapolis Foundation when he was quoted in the paper saying, "Most One Percent Club members don't need the advice of the Minneapolis Foundation." I happened to be a member of the One Percent Club and find the advice and service provided by the Minneapolis Foundation to be invaluable. When I questioned Joe on his quote, his response was, "These are my own honest perceptions." End of subject.

Joe is a bulldog; he never gives up. Recently five of us met with him to discuss a particularly important issue. After two hours of discussion, the vote was 5 to 1 against proceeding on Joe's proposal. The next day Joe called me and wanted a recount. I had to hang up on him. It doesn't matter if you are friend or foe, Joe tells you exactly how he feels and exactly what is on his mind.

With Joe Selvaggio, what you see is what you get—and I love him and am one of his greatest fans. He has made a difference in my life and the lives of many, many others. I would suspect, however, he will not ask me to make a comment for his next book. And yet, he might. He's not a guy to blanch at frankness.

Richard McFarland is the retired CEO of Dain Rauscher.

From Joe's letters to Sam:

Dear Sam:

In the spring of 2003 I came close to quitting as the Executive Director of the One Percent Club. The crisis arose over the issue of "who should be a member?"

I contended that "high-net-worth" people should be members. The board of directors wanted *anyone* to be a member, and argued that we should drop the phrase "people of means" from the mission statement.

They said we should not appear to be "targeting" the rich. We should not "rub their noses in their wealth" by using terms like "people of means." We should be inclusive, not "classist."

I argued that the club was inspired by the book *Wealthy and Wise* by Claude Rosenberg, Jr., who was not afraid to use the word "wealthy." What's wrong with being rich? Our very name—"One Percent"—refers to one percent of accumulated wealth. Middle income and low-income folks, by definition, don't have much accumulated wealth. We'd already settled for the least offensive phrase after discarding a long list of words like rich, wealthy, affluent, high-net-worth… Let's be honest and open about who should be in the club, I argued, even though we won't refuse anybody who wants to join. After all, when Willie Sutton was asked why he robbed banks he said, "Because that's where the money is." The real purpose of the One Percent Club is to get more money into the hands of non-profits. Going to the top of the financial pyramid can do this most efficiently and effectively. There are 6000 families in Minnesota worth $5 million or more. That's where the money is. It's a big enough job to concentrate on them without diluting our efforts. Besides, it's a matter of justice, and it's been proven that middle income and the poor already give generously.

But, when it came to a vote, I lost. The board decided to drop the phrase "people of means."

When I informed certain members of the board that I had no interest in being executive director of a club whose purpose was to encourage the generosity of all (as opposed to focusing on the wealthy), one person in particular got mad at me. He accused me of "taking my ball and going home" because I couldn't get my way. That person was Dr. Ford Watson Bell, former chair of the board and a person I very much loved and respected. I hated to lose a friend and working partner like Ford. I hated the thought of losing other friends on the board. But this was business, not personal. This was about how I wanted to spend the remaining days of my work-life. I had to be faithful to my own priorities, my own dreams. When we had gotten the headline story in the Sunday edition of the *Star Tribune* (which we got because all of the club members were prominent millionaires), I thought I had died and gone to heaven. My career was complete. But now my dream was being taken away from me by removing the phrase "people of means" from the mission. The Club was substantively changed. I felt that I had no choice but to leave.

But it wasn't to be that simple. Just as I was about to turn in my resignation, I received notification that I had been awarded the first Louis W. Hill, Jr. Award through the Hubert H. Humphrey Institute of Public Affairs. A total shock. With this award came the responsibility of giving a big lecture at the end of the year, on philanthropy, community, or leadership. It was pretty obvious I'd won because of my work with the One Percent Club. If I quit, people would be dismayed, research would be hampered, and a bad taste would be left in everyone's mouth.

My friend Ford Bell had also threatened to resign over this issue. The clear answer to the situation was for both of us to give up some of our demands and stay. If either one of us left, I could see the club starting to crumble.

I went to see Ford at his office at the Minneapolis Heart Institute Foundation. I laid my cards out on the table. Ford, fair man that he is, thought for a half a second and agreed. Both of us would stay. We would "keep the peace—keep the unity."

Ben Franklin, the artful master of compromise, would have been proud of us.

Love,

Dad

Dear Sam,

I've told you about how I got started in my social service/advocacy career after leaving the priesthood. In 1969 I sent a letter asking 200 of my friends if they would send me a modest check (between $5 and $25 per month) so I could quit my job selling mutual funds at IDS and work as an extension of them in the areas of race, peace and poverty. One hundred of them said "Yes," in effect buying stock *in me* rather than in some corporation, and I worked for them for three years—the three years before Ted Pouliot and I started PPL.

I've also told you how I financed the last few years of my career in a similar fashion. But rather than having 100 families support me, I got 13 families to give $5000 per year for my $50,000 per year salary plus expenses. As I approached retirement, I sensed the families were getting tired of supporting me, so my friend Mike Winton agreed to send a letter to my supporters asking for one final gift.

Here's the letter Mike sent in the spring of 2002 to wind up my support through PPL.

> Dear _______________ (e.g., Kenneth Dayton):
>
> You and I are part of a group providing Joe Selvaggio's salary. I do, however, want to thank you for contributing to the community's well-being through Joe's work. You and I know how much good has followed from Joe's efforts. Our contribution may be indirect, but it enables Joe to devote full time to pursuits he, uniquely, is able to perform. Besides the reports we receive through his and Jim Scheibel's quarterly letters, PPL's newsletter, and the One Percent Club's monthly newsletter, I'm sure you've personally encountered evidences of his fine work. In short, I think we can confidently assert that we've gotten our money's worth from our $5000 annual contribution.
>
> For thirty years I have been urging Joe to negotiate a decent retirement package from PPL so he could have sufficient retirement income and continue his service as a volunteer. For years he has resisted, saying that he did not want to burden PPL with more overhead. While his strategy has been morally edifying, as we look closely at his retirement needs of approximately $30,000 per year after income taxes, we see that he needs to have another $50,000 in his 403-B retirement account.

I am proposing that some of us (or all of us) "chip in" on a one-time basis to fund this $50,000 need. This will definitely wind up our commitment to fund Joe's work, which he will be able to continue long into the future—as long as he is able. As you will recall, we presently have one more $5000 payment due by the end of this year (or early next year) for Joe's work to be done in 2003. If each of us would simply give $10,000 rather than $5000, both our final payment and the one-time contribution to the $50,000 fund could be done together. If some are not willing to contribute, that's fine. The rest of us will try to figure out a way to fund the $50,000 one-time problem.

This would also solve another problem. The twelve funders of Joe's salary are also funders of PPL, and in some cases the One Percent Club. With PPL starting a capital campaign and the One Percent Cub and PPL having general operating needs, these competing claims become confusing to funders. Cleaning this up as soon as possible is in the best interest of all.

Although I hate to tap your generosity one more time, I feel compelled to write this letter and ask for your consideration. Thus I am enclosing a sheet for you to fill out and return, to my attention, in the enclosed envelope. Whatever you decide, know that I, Jim Scheibel, and Joe Selvaggio will be pleased and grateful for your generosity to our community.

Sincerely,

Mike Winton
CC: Joe Selvaggio & Jim Scheibel

Rose calls me a beggar for making my living this way, but as long as the funders are willing to do it, and I can work hard and effectively, I have no problem with it. And I could never bring myself to diverting PPL funds intended to help the poor to fund a pension for me or anyone else at PPL. I've seen too many such enterprises undermined by the greed or selfishness of those who ran them. Call me a naive moron, but at least I'm not taking the bread out of some kid's mouth.

Much love,

Dad

12. The Will to Work

Joe Selvaggio: Poverty Inc.

by Steve Rothschild

Joe Selvagggio is known as "St. Joe" by many in the community, but the only religion he worships is the almighty dollar. Who else would start three non-profits to line his own pockets? Only a tiny fraction of the millions Joe has raised over the years has made its way to PPL or the One Percent Club. The rest has gone to buying villas in Mexico and Cuba, his favorite destination spots.

Joe loves taking money from the rich because he despises anyone who has more money than he has. It's so difficult to elude Joe's "pick-pocket hands" that I've found it best to keep him close by. I had to sew my wallet in my right front pocket, though.

Joe badgered me so long to write an article for his book that I decided to tell the truth. In fact, "writing" the book is just another one of his schemes, since everybody in town but Joe is doing the work!

[Steve Rothschild sent those three clearly facetious paragraphs (well, maybe the third paragraph isn't entirely facetious) to Joe just to yank his chain a bit. That he did so testifies not only to Steve's wry sense of humor, but also Joe's wonderful ability to genuinely enjoy a laugh at his own expense. Rothschild describes how he really feels about Joe Selvaggio in the paragraphs that follow.—Ed.]

Twin Cities RISE! and Joe.

I met Joe Selvaggio in 1993, shortly after I left the corporate world. He was introduced to me by a mutual friend, Chuck Denny, retired CEO of ADC Telecommunications. I was exploring the possibility of beginning a non-profit devoted to boosting the hardest-to-employ out of poverty. I had concluded that, despite the multitude of social services and billions of dollars being spent, that too few women who left welfare actually escaped poverty, and that there was virtually nothing available for the least-prepared and poorest men. This was particularly true for African Americans and Native Americans who experienced the worst "generational poverty." Our social service and educational "system" had a large gap—not unlike a school system that didn't offer eighth through twelfth grades.

The cruel irony of this predicament is that at the very time many economically poor people were falling farther behind, employers were increasingly seeking skilled people of color to reflect their changing customer base and to meet overall demand.

Joe impressed me as that rare individual who was constantly creating new solutions for the toughest social problems while also possessing the discipline, analytical ability and common sense to get things done. He was both encouraging and challenging of my ideas. He agreed to join a fledgling steering committee that was helping to develop the project and to introduce me to his valuable contacts in the philanthropic, governmental and social service communities.

It's easy to underestimate Joe when you first meet him. His slight build, soft voice and gentle demeanor belie a steel backbone, critical eye and courageous soul that speaks out for those who can't speak for themselves.

As I began to plan in earnest, Michael Patton, the brilliant evaluator, convinced me to develop principles, not lots of procedures or rules, "since all the evidence suggests that we'd have to change it lots of times before we got it right." Joe chuckled and agreed.

The four key principles based upon which we developed Twin Cities RISE! (and still abide by) are:

1. The only customers are the employers, since they have the jobs. It is their needs and standards that we must focus on in order to benefit our participants. Our responsibility is to train the participants so they can successfully negotiate with an employer for a living-wage job that pays benefits.
2. Focus on the hardest to employ, because they are underserved. Our population is 90 percent people of color, 70 percent of whom are African-American. All are economically poor. The average educational competency is seventh grade. Half have criminal backgrounds and two thirds have abused drugs or alcohol.

   These are traditional "throw-away workers," whom our economy now needs as we face a demographics-driven labor shortage over the next 15 to 20 years as baby boomers retire. It also makes sense to invest in people's skill development instead of subsidizing them. It makes ethical, social and economic sense.
3. Each stakeholder, including participant, government, employer and TCR! must be accountable based on the value that it receives in order for the model to be sustainable. As such, we charge employers a fee based on the turnover costs they avoid by hiring our graduates, who are retained on the job longer (our experience is 85 percent one-year and 79 percent two-year retention). We also developed a unique "pay-for-performance model" with the State of Minnesota in which we are rewarded for placements and retentions, based on the increased tax revenue and decreased public subsidies that the state derives from our moving poor individuals up the income ladder. The State only pays for successes, thereby eliminating its risk. The State's return on investment could approach $4.00 for each $1.00 it spends. We are working on a similar model with the Federal government, as well.

   After an eight-week trial period, participants sign an agreement that obligates them to work for one year after graduation for free tuition and support costs, akin to an ROTC grant. Justice Brandeis is reported to have told his granddaughter that "life is not easy, and the sooner you find that out, the easier it will be." Learning the ways of the world that participants will enter are important lessons during the program.

Twin Cities RISE! is accountable, too, because it earns revenue only if it is successful in placing and retaining individuals in jobs paying a living wage. Without success, we disappear; with it, we grow. In 1995 we served 19 individuals. This year we will serve over 600. And at placement, our average graduate will have increased his earnings by over 150 percent to more than $23,000 plus benefits.

4. Each individual develops "from the inside out." While we teach technical skills and basic skills, we have found that each participant needs to embrace accountability for his or her own development before real learning can take place. This is a particular hurdle for those who have lived in generational poverty where victimization, entitlement and powerlessness are coping behaviors. TCR!'s empowerment curriculum pervades the organization's culture. Empowered individuals control their emotions, deal with conflict and solve problems. Many a participant has told me that "I came here for a better job, but this is really about changing my life." We attribute our excellent retention results to our focus on empowerment.

Throughout TCR!'s history Joe has remained a steadfast sounding board and supporter. The only thing he has refused to do is give me his "A" donor list or do active fundraising for us. Our most productive times are spent walking around Lake Harriet. Joe's brain seems to work better when his feet are moving! He has saved me from more than one bad idea, and I have had a chance to critique some of his many editorials. As I seek some way to sum-up the value Joe has brought to our community I recall the following lines from T. E. Lawrence's *Seven Pillars of Wisdom*:

"ALL MEN DREAM: but not equally. Those who dream by night in the dusty recesses of their minds wake in the day to find that it was vanity. But the dreamers of the day are dangerous men, for they may act their dream with open eyes, to make it possible."

Steve Rothschild, formerly executive vice president of the Yoplait division of General Mills, is the founder and Chairman of the Board of Twin Cities RISE!

Joe Is Quiet, But He's Tough

by John Hartwell

In 1987, after I sold my business, I decided to volunteer at a nonprofit that helped people learn to work. My friend and former CEO of ADC Telecommunications, Chuck Denny, told me that he had had a wonderful experience chairing the board of directors of PPL Industries, a job-training program for disadvantaged folks in the core city of Minneapolis. This nonprofit work program had two mottoes: "Creating dignity through work," and "Give me a fish and I eat for a day; teach me to fish and I eat for a lifetime." He emphasized that it was run like a business, and that if I wanted to get involved, I should get to know Joe Selvaggio.

In due time I set up an interview with Joe, during which I got to know him a bit and he had a chance to tell me about PPL. My initial impression was hat he was really soft-spoken and low-key, but he also had a deep desire to improve the lives of poor people. I was very impressed by the wonderful work that PPL was doing in providing jobs and housing for inner-city people.

I was asked to join the PPL Board of Directors, and then Joe and I had a discussion about what he and the organization expected from me. I thought that I made it clear to him that I was willing to help in many ways, but the one area in which I did *not* want to be involved was fundraising.

My initial involvement with PPL was on the SHOP (Surplus Home and Office Products) committee. I worked hard with the SHOP, which thanks to the efforts of Sue Jaqua and others has grown dramatically and become very successful. In those early years, I had lots of contact with Joe Selvaggio. I realized more than ever how intense his motivation was to help poor people. If there was a chance to help a number of people in need, he was willing to take some pretty big risks.

In the early 1990s is became quite clear that PPL needed to embark on a capital campaign. The goal of the campaign was to raise about $5 million. I couldn't believe it when Joe asked me to co-chair the campaign with him. I asked him to think back to our first meeting, when I had told him that the one thing I did not want to do was raise money. I urged him to get someone else, but he insisted that he needed me. I said that I needed some time to think about it.

Joe continued to apply his gentle pressure, and as those who know him would have predicted, I agreed to lead the campaign along with this quiet salesman.

Joe was wonderful to work with, and throughout the effort I got to know him even better. Through consistent and gentle prodding, he encouraged me to make contacts that were a bit uncomfortable, with people I didn't know well. The campaign was a success, and I was amazed at how many generous and caring people there are in the Twin Cities. Thanks to Joe, I also learned that raising money wasn't as unpleasant a task as I had thought.

Joe is a great fund-raiser. He has no fear of going to corporate leaders and asking for money. He has an unusual ability to work hand-in-hand helping poor people improve their lives while simultaneously cultivating comfortable relationships with the Twin Cities' top corporate executives. I think this is because he believes so strongly in the PPL motto about teaching men to fish.

Joe is quiet, but he's tough. He pinches pennies with the best. He also loses patience trying to help people who aren't willing to work to help themselves.

I had another interesting experience with Joe in the early '90s. We were having lunch one day, and we agreed that PPL was not as well know in the Twin Cities as it should be. We talked about ways to change that, and we came up with the idea of a Greyhound bus tour of some of PPL's many facilities and activities. When it came to deciding who would get people to take the tour, Joe suggested that I might be a good candidate, and, sure enough, I agreed.

I wasn't easy to get people to agree to meet at the Minneapolis Club, hop on a bus at 4:00 p.m. for a tour that would last about two-and-a-half hours, and stay for refreshments and a white-tablecloth dinner served in the old Northeast Minneapolis warehouse that houses the SHOP. Nevertheless, through mailed invitations and lots of telephone calls we rustled up 44 people to fill the bus.

The bus trip was great fun, and lots of new people were exposed to the good things that PPL does. Many of those individuals and couples have become regular donors to the organization. Joe is full of ideas, and that bus trip was one of the very good ones.

I have now known Joe Selvaggio for more than 15 years, and I love him. He has done, and continues to do, wonderful and caring things for the Twin Cities community.

John Hartwell is the retired CEO of Land-O-Nod Mattress company and a community volunteer and philanthropist.

From Joe's letters to Sam

Dear Sam,

Almost every month I go to a graduation ceremony at PPL. These ceremonies changed my thinking from "all a poor person needs is an opportunity to work" to "poor people and work atmospheres need to be 'job-ready.'" We need a strong economy with plenty of jobs at all levels. I agree with the statement, "The best welfare program is a good job."

But that slogan doesn't tell the whole story. Some folks are not ready to hold a job. And for those, we need what they call in the trade, a "work-readiness" program.

At PPL I think we have the best work-readiness program in the country. You can see it if you attend the graduation ceremonies at Abbott Northwestern Hospital. At the ceremony 10 to 15 "poor people" stand up and tell their stories. One might say, "six years ago I was in the battle zone of Somalia not knowing if I'd get hit by a bullet or a bomb. Today I stand before you—safe, trained as a medical records keeper, and hopeful for a great future."

The next person might say something like, "Last year I was getting into the gang scene in Gary, Indiana. You know what I mean? Now I'm trained as a maintenance man. I thank my mama for moving me from Gary to Minneapolis. I thank God. I thank Abbott Northwestern Hospital for hiring me, and I thank PPL for giving me the training and the right attitude. I'm on my way. You know what I'm sayin'?"

Sometimes I'm asked to speak at their graduation. I get to tell them about my father who came to this country with a fourth grade education—how he had disadvantages, but his determination and hard work allowed him to make money and give a better life to his kids.

Once I brought Tony Bouza with me and he gave a little speech. He told them that he was an immigrant coming here from Spain at 9 years old. But he studied hard and competed in civil service tests allowing him to become chief of police here in Minneapolis. Tony told of his mother, who worked as a seamstress. Sometimes when she was tired she'd drive a needle through a fingernail. But the pain didn't stop her. She'd bandage her finger and go on sewing. Life is *tough* for most people.

When Arthur Ashe, the great tennis star was asked if he could cope with the AIDS virus he had contacted through a blood transfusion, Ash said something like, "It will be tough, but there's nothing tougher than growing up black in America." Tony Bouza would tell them, sure, life will be tough, especially if you're black, but you've got to ask yourself if you want to be a *victor*, or a *victim*.

Graduation days are always happy. Family shows up to cheer, inspirational speeches abound, cake and punch make it festive. But some hard work had to be done to earn the graduation.

The students had to get up every morning—even cold snowy mornings when their bodies craved to stay in bed. They had to walk a few blocks to the bus—sometimes in snow without proper footwear. Once they have arrived at the hospital they attended some classes but also visited their potential work sites. The student who didn't speak English very well and never had much schooling might feel more comfortable making the beds and delivering the meals. Another student who preferred office work might choose to sit by a receptionist and learn that job. After the visit to the job site, where the student could get the feel of the job and judge whether it might be a good fit, the student would then go to a class.

The classes revolved around resume writing, grooming, and having the right attitude to get along with the patients and the co-workers. Their activities, which lasted for four weeks, may sound easy for youth raised in middle class families. But for a person brought in recently from a war-torn country or a person who never held a job, they can be quite challenging.

Why do I say that our program is the best in the country? Because our retention rate is 80 percent. That means that 80 percent of those who graduate and accept jobs are still on the job a year later. It's not easy. In fact we need to have two full-time retention specialists working with the new workers to keep them motivated—to keep them working after they have run-ins with their boss, or get irritated by a cranky patient. You can't just toss them out there to drift downstream alone.

The program is not cheap. It costs $500,000 to graduate every 200 students, or $2500 per student. But the cost is a great bargain to society compared to the cost of supporting students who do not graduate. Without being trained to work, some of these folks would incur welfare, jail, and broken family costs estimated to be triple our costs.

And that doesn't count the positive wealth that these folks create when they are changed from poor to middle class. Workers produce wealth by their work. It's not just goods in the earth (trees, oil, water) that produce wealth. Lots of poor countries have those resources. But only the countries that have learned how to get their people working—hard and smart—really prosper. The development of human recourses needs to be unlocked. Motivation and education are the keys.

We, as taxpayers or philanthropists, should be wise enough to pay for it. In the short run, it looks pricey. In the long run, it's a great bargain.

Love,

Dad

P.S. I was talking recently to Sopha Nhep of Best Steak & Gyros. When he lived in Cambodia as a youth, his family of 15 people had to divide a single chicken among them to eat. Then he saw a Clint Eastwood movie in which Eastwood took a bite of a chicken and threw the rest away. At that moment he decided he wanted to live in a country that was so rich its citizens could throw away food.

13. "The Arc of a Life."

From the play *Joe*

Joe told me a story about someone who was acting insecure and another observer said of them, "He must have been stepped on early in life." … Then Joe said, "I was never stepped on. That was just unthinkable." Imagine being brought up to know—not just to believe, but to *know*—that you will never be stepped on. How wonderful. Joe said, "I just knew that I would be OK because of my mother's and father's love. And my Aunts' and my Uncles'…"

We've Come a Long Way

by Ted Pouliot

In PPL's early days, *everyone* got involved in grass-roots projects. Try to imagine Joe wielding a paintbrush, *himself*. He would join Evelyn Franklin, Gertrude Esteros, my wife, and me—even Mary Fraser (daughter of former Congressman and Minneapolis mayor Don and Arvonne)—in performing all the tasks involved in restoring inner-city houses. During PPL's first eight exciting years, when I was board chairman, neither Joe nor I envisioned the organization's growing to its present size.

We started working in the Phillips neighborhood in south Minneapolis. Our biggest problem was in trying to work with the Phillips Neighborhood Improvement Association (PNIA). PNIA was irritated with PPL because we had a HUD (Housing and Urban Development) grant from the federal government to do some research and planning for the neighborhood. Since PNIA was the official neighborhood group, they wanted to control the way the grant money was spent. When we resisted, they wanted to take control of PPL, or at least get the federal grant transferred to them. We had many lunches with PNIA representatives and tried to work together, but in the end they tried to pressure the city council to disapprove PPL as a licensed contractor.

Our board meetings were open, and at one, PNIA members turned out in force with reporters and TV cameras. Calling me the "carpetbagger from the suburbs," they almost succeeded in ruining our relationship with the Minneapolis City Council and with HUD officials, but in the end, Joe calmed everyone down, the city sided with PPL, and PNIA faded away.

Beyond our PPL relationship, Joe and I have had a long-standing personal relationship. Joe has officiated at family weddings and funerals. When Joe agreed to help Rose Escañan escape from Ferdinand Marcos's wrath by agreeing to marry her, I agreed to help. I had a factory in Manila that I visited twice a year, so it was easy for me to arrange secret meetings with Rose. It became my job to arrange for her ticket and verify that she understood that a divorce would take place after she'd been in the U.S. for six months.

Joe married Rose as soon as she arrived in the United States. Two weeks later, Joe and his girlfriend went on vacation with my wife and me to Maui, Hawaii. Imagine trying to explain to our Maui friends that Joe had married a Filipina two weeks ago, but was now on vacation with his girlfriend. That was another first for Joe.

Joe and Rose have now been married for nearly 20 years. What a way to get a great wife!

My wife, Mary Jo, and I spend the month of February painting in Mexico with other artists. Joe and Rose have joined us several times. Joe said if he had to paint it would be of the derrières of Mexican beauties walking the beach. Maybe Joe will advance to painting full figures in his retirement.

Joe now advises me regarding an adult education school I support in Haiti. (Even in fourth-world countries, Joe likes to drive. Imagine getting lost in the slums of Port-au- Prince, Haiti!) I've worked in China two months a year to support this project. The rest of the money has come through referrals from Joe.

Joe is still my best friend, and we have had so many experiences together, both in Minnesota and overseas, that I could write a book—but that's *his* job.

Ted Pouliot, retired CEO of Pouliot Design, was the founding board chairman of Project for Pride in Living. Currently he is a painter.

You Bastard!

by Dan Turner

I've known Joe for 45 years. We entered the seminary together to study for the priesthood and have remained friends since then, much to my wonderment and pain. We haven't lived together since ordination, much to my joy. And both of us left the priesthood to pursue careers in social justice. We have traveled together in Central America, during the wars there in the 1980s and '90s. In 1995, we pilgrimaged throughout the Philippines with a group of Buddhist monks who commemorated the 50th anniversary of the end of World War II by going to places of battle and cemeteries to pray for the fallen soldiers and civilians.

Joe's work has inspired me and—I hate to say this—caused me to admire him immensely. That is one of the pains he gives me. He is the kind of person who makes me laugh to tears and then drives me to screeching anger as he whines, wheedles and cajoles me to agree with him on some maddening point in politics or theology. His patience is not a virtue but a weapon to overcome one's reluctance to agree with him over some issue or course of action.

But enough of this. Joe tells terrible jokes well. One time I met him at a department store and he starts telling me a story as we descend the escalator. It takes me a while to catch on it's a joke and then he hits me with a punch line that sends me sprawling down the steps and grabbing onto the moving handrail so I don't seriously damage myself. He stands behind me softly chuckling. (For the sake of readers who have been brought up decently, I dare not divulge his jokes).

Another time, Joe, my wife Elizabeth and I were in a mountain village in El Salvador. Fr. Jim Barnett, a classmate of ours and a courageous apostle to the people, took us there to meet the villagers and hear their stories of the terrible war that was being waged against them. At night Joe, Elizabeth and I slept in hammocks with a family in their small casa. There were a mother, her sister and three little kids. It was a clear black, dark night. A sense of peace had settled on us. The murmur of the mother quieting her children was soporific.I was just about to drift off when Joe says, "I got a joke."

"Shut up and go to sleep, Joe."

"No, it's too good. I hafta tell you." So he starts. I notice the mother stops talking as we're speaking. Joe tells the funniest story I have ever heard. The three of us explode in laughter and then try to muffle our screams so as not to disturb the family, but they start laughing too. I can hear the children's sweet giggling, even though they don't understand English. For five minutes the hammocks swing furiously and every one is in a helpless state of spasm. Finally, we calm down. My last, quiet words to Joe that night are: "You bastard."

I think that's a good word to end on. He sure is one ... but a damn good one.

Dan Turner is a writer living in Oakland, California, as far away from Joe as he can get.

From Joe's letters to Sam

Dear Sam,

You may know some of this, but certainly not all. I'll try to give you a sense of the "arc of my life," but I'll leave out stories I know you've already heard.

Do I have a desire to write this sort of personal story? Hardly. I'm doing it because my editor and my 15 test-reader friends tell me I need to. "The reader of your book needs an overview of who you are, what you've experienced, how you think." When that many smart people tell me something, I sense they may be right, but that doesn't make it any easier to do what they want. I have an instinctual revulsion to writing an overview of my life. It feels like a mini-memoir, and the "memoir phenomenon" has gotten way out of hand. The public may want to know more about the lives of celebrities, but of every "Joe Schmo" who comes along? I doubt it. Besides, I'm like the guy who said, "I'd write a memoir if I could remember what happened."

I thought of saying, "screw you" to my editor and test-readers. That's what one of my heroes, George Carlin, would say. But since I don't have the money or the talent to go it alone, I'll repress my instinct, be a good soldier, and go along.

• • •

I was born of an immigrant father who came over from Bari, Italy, with a 4th grade education. My mother might just as well have been born in Italy, since both her parents were born there, and they sheltered her to the extent that she felt far more Italian than American. She used to say, "If kittens are born in the oven, they don't call them cookies."

My only sibling, your uncle John, who was four years older than I (but still only 61 when he died of a heart attack) took after my father: brash, cocky, and aggressive. I was more like my mother: quiet, accommodating, and mellow (some would say lazy, since they called me "slow-motion" and "step-and-fetch-it" as a boy).

I attended a Catholic grade school in Chicago, where the Sisters talked enough nunsense to me about eternal hell-fire to keep me a virgin—without even a single instance of "self-abuse"—until I was 30 years old; quite a feat for a hot-blooded Italian boy.

My early years were spent growing up over my dad's awning shop at 5443 Division St., a street Studs Terkel, a Chicago writer, made famous with his book, *Division Street: America.* Many summer hours were spent sitting on a 4 x 4 x 4 foot cement triangle built into a neighbor's commercial building in our alley. What I mediated on, I have no idea. But, cumulatively, I spent months, if not years, perched 10 feet up there, watching the cars and delivery trucks drive by during the hot summer days.

Many boys my age, I'm told, "played doctor" with a girl their age. The best I could do was to watch the little sister of my friend perform a silly fast dance, *naked,* in the window of the apartment next door to our awning shop. Since I had no sisters, and my puritanical Catholic upbringing forbade even photos of naked females, those occasional dances were the highlights of my early years.

As I got older and attended our neighborhood Catholic school, I played the normal sports in those days: baseball (mostly 16-inch softball), football, and basketball. No soccer, hockey, or tennis. Our baseball team was called the *Dominoes*. I can still remember the names and positions of the whole team: Conlin at shortstop, Murphy at first base, Mulligan at second base… just like I can still remember the names and positions of the 1945 pennant-winning Chicago Cubs: Smalley at shortstop, Caveretta at first base, Johnson at second base…

My grammar school friends were, by and large, children of immigrants from Ireland, Germany, Poland, and Italy. Their mothers were full-time mothers, and the fathers were breadwinners, often absent from any relationships with their children. I knew only one kid whose mother was divorced. Of course she could not re-marry, because if she did, she would be excommunicated from her beloved Catholic Church.

When my brother and I saw *The Deerhunter*, a movie with Meryl Streep and Robert DeNiro, my brother said to me, "Wow, those are exactly the kind of kids we grew up with in Chicago." I agreed. Our fathers were mostly blue-collar workers, and we considered ourselves part of the community of hard-working American-Catholic families. As grammar-school friends we were very close.

Even today, some of my closest friends are the friends I made in grammar school. Life was simpler back in the forties. Whenever we have re-unions, we can talk with a comfortable ease. It is as if we have not been separated for decades. Would that every child had a childhood so happy.

My nuclear family included my mother, Mary, a gentle soul. I never heard her say "shit," "hell," or "damn"—probably because she never said those words. My father, Sam, (who was baptized "Savario" but changed it to be more American.) had a more volatile personality and used much spicier language. "Dirty bastard" and a few Italian vulgarities came out of his mouth daily. Then my aunt, Helen Mascari, lived with us. She was my mother's younger sister (by one year). Since she never married, and, for most years, never worked outside the home, it was like having two mothers. Her love was unconditional and appreciated, but her presence made it twice as difficult to get away with anything. She would often say, "Wouldn't it be nice if everyone were nice?" My brother, John, being the older sibling, never let me doubt who was boss. Once, at an Italian picnic, John showed some interest in the daughter of a Mafia member, but my mother put a stop to that in a hurry. An uncle, Joe, also lived with us (until he got married) in the three-bedroom apartment above the shop. As far as I can recall, we all got along well.

We lived on a streetcar line, so the clangy noise of the cars was continual. Every spring we would participate in a "Division Street Parade." All of my friends would come over and we'd pile into the back of my dad's red 1937 Plymouth Awning truck, and we'd toss out match books with *West Side Awning Co*. printed on them. There was a caricature of the sun with tears coming out of its eyes on the side of the truck and on the matchbook covers, with the words, "We make him weep" inscribed under the sun.

My mother had six living siblings, five of whom resided in the Chicago area. That led to many picnics and holiday parties, where stories were told of a seventh sibling, John, who was shot dead by a brother with a loaded handgun in a tragic accident when he was nine years old.

One of my mother's brothers, Frank, was a dentist. Uncle Frank was the star in the family—the only one (in his generation) who played college football, had *finished* college and become a professional. He was a dapper dresser, sported a neatly trimmed mustache, had a big house in the suburb of River Forest, and a nice wife, Gen, with two children, Jeannie, and Joe. Jeannie was two years older than I, and a beautiful girl. If she weren't my older cousin I'd have found a way to hustle her. Joe was two years younger—a likable kid, and acted like the little brother I never had.

We had other uncles, aunts and cousins—the Giuffres, the Franciones, the Notaros, but I'd rather tell you their stories in person. Suffice it to say, it was a wonderful extended family—no abuse, no poverty, and no burning family feuds—not a bad way to grow up.

• • •

My high school years were spent at a Catholic school (Fenwick) in a suburb (Oak Park). There I was exposed to some rich kids from the western suburbs of Chicago. I've never been able to stop comparing the privileged lives of my high school classmates with the sparse lives of my inner-city neighbors and youth in Minneapolis. The contrasts are vivid, and they're always stimulating me to try to figure out how to get more for the poor without threatening to take away too much from the rich.

Experiences in high school didn't help much in choosing a career, but they did help me eliminate some careers (those in sports). One of the prime motivations I had for choosing Fenwick was the fact that they had the best football team among the city's Catholic schools. In grammar school we used to climb over the fence at Hanson stadium and watch the two Barrett brothers, Ed LaJune, and Johnny Lattner (who later played college football at Notre Dame and won the Heisman trophy in 1953) run crowd-pleasing touchdowns demolishing the opposition. I dreamed of wearing one of those sharp black and white uniforms and playing on a championship team.

When I got to high school there were try-outs for the team during the first week of school. For two days I raced, caught passes, threw passes, and tried to impress the coaches. On Friday they were to announce on the bulletin board who made the team. I anxiously awaited the typed sheet. When I stepped up to the bulletin board with about 20 other students I read the list once, twice, three times. There must be a mistake. My name wasn't on the list. How could that happen? A tough Chicago kid got beat out by these soft suburban kids? No way. Impossible!

But the bottom line finally sank in. This city kid was just not big enough, not fast enough, just plain not good enough to make the team. I was devastated. My years of anticipation were dashed by some stinking typed piece of paper without my name on it.

The second cold shower of reality came during the boxing season. I won one fight and got a chance to size up the other contenders in my weight class. There were only two boys who looked rather good. Oddly enough, they were two of the darkest-skinned boys in the school. They weren't Negroes, as we called them then, but one looked Mexican and the taller one with the long reach looked East Indian.

My next fight was with the gangly guy. I thought I was stronger than he, so I should be able to overpower him and then get on to the tougher, stockier, Mexican-looking kid.

I entered the ring a bit nervous, but the traditional wisdom said that everyone is nervous at first… "It goes away with the first punch." We danced around a bit and then the first punch came. He jabbed me a couple more times—I tried to get in closer, but his long arm with a fist on the end kept knocking me in the head every time I approached. Then a flurry of fists came at me—bam! bam! bam! Before I knew it I was on the ropes and the ref was calling it a TKO. My pride was again in the toilet. But it got worse. The next day the Mexican kid beat the crap out of the gangly kid. A sugar Ray Robinson (or Oscar de la Hoya for you younger folks) I was not. My boxing ambitions were over.

Then came the spring, with try-outs for the golf team. My sights were lowering fast but, as it turned out, not fast enough. The first day we gathered in the gym to hear the coach announce, "We have too many kids here. If you haven't been shooting, consistently, under 100 on tough courses, I don't want to see you on the course tomorrow. That's the bar. Let's not waste each other's time." Hell, I had a hard time breaking 100 on the small Park courses. My golfing career ended before it even started.

During the evenings some of us would often go over to the Dwyer girls' house. The twins, Peggy and Patty Dwyer, were not only good looking and well-built, but they had a mother who genuinely liked to talk to us. One evening Mrs. Dwyer said to me, "Joe, what do you think you'd like to do with your life"?

I answered, "Oh, I'll probably just take over my dad's awning business."

"But what do you *really* want to do? What are you passionate about? What do you enjoy doing? Don't sell yourself short. What are your dreams"?

"Well, what I'd really like to do," I responded, "is to be a professional athlete—maybe a baseball player, a basketball player, even a golf or tennis star."

Then I remembered my try-outs for football, boxing, and golf. "Man, I've got to be realistic. Who would pay to see me play when there are so many who can play better than I can"? I asked myself. The truth hurts, and it hurt me more because I was young. But realism is still the better path. It's good that I eliminated sports as a viable career at an early age (or that they eliminated me.)

• • •

College took me to the Jesuits at Marquette University, in Milwaukee. There my defining moment came during my third year, when I got a call from my mother saying that my father had had a stroke, and that I was needed back home to run the family business. This temporary dropout (my father recovered from the stroke to resume running the business) led me to know that I did not want spend the rest of my life trying to sell people canvas awnings. Instead, after a summer of soul-searching, I chose to sell people on living the virtuous life by joining the Order of Preachers (the Dominicans), and eventually becoming a priest. Back then getting a "higher place in heaven," for eternity, was the clear motivator. Now, the "heaven thing" is never a motivator for the decisions I make.

My three years at Marquette University, in the heart of Milwaukee, are a bit of a blur. The friendships I made there were not nearly as strong as the friendships I had in grammar school and high school. I didn't like the courses I took. My brother talked me into studying engineering—something I had no interest in. After two years of engineering I switched into liberal arts and became a Math major, simply because I wanted to graduate in four years, and I had all these Math credits from engineering.

One pivotal event occurred during the spring of my third year of college, in a visit I had from Father Jacobs, a teacher I'd had at Fenwick. I had talked to Fr. Jacobs about a possible vocation to the priesthood when I went home to run my dad's business. One Saturday morning, out of the blue, Fr. Jacobs showed up at the door of my apartment—the top floor of a three-story mansion in the fraternity row area of Marquette. It was 10 a.m. and all four of us roommates were sleeping in. The night before our apartment had been the location of a raucous party, and when I opened the door for the priest, the stench of cigarettes and stale beer almost knocked him down the stairs. After a few jibes at my life-style, he asked me out for breakfast to talk about my vocation. I felt he was a pretty cool priest for not tossing me out of the running because of the stink and party-look of the apartment.

• • •

When I joined the Order in August of 1958, I was 21 years old. A Dominican priest, Fr. Irwin, drove four of us up from Chicago, Illinois to Winona, Minnesota. For some reason I, John McCarthy, Gerry Malizia, and a young Nordic-looking man had to arrive a week late. We had our black suits and white shirts on and had a reasonable amount of anxiety.

As soon as we got there we were given religious names. I lucked out and was given the name *Brother Anthony*, and Malizia was given the name *Brother Andrew*.

I could tell Malizia was a bit envious because he was from a very Italian family and Andrew was not as Italian as Anthony. McCarthy got the first name of *Timothy*—very Irish, and the young Viking looking man got the name *Brother Eric*. I could tell he was happy. We quickly met twenty-six other *postulants*, as we were called for the 10 days before we took the religious habit.

Our class of 30, rather large for those days, was congenial. I guess we were all on our best behavior with high motivation to please the Lord by pleasing our superiors and existing in harmony with our new religious brothers. In fact, *harmony* was the goal. We were told that the end of religious life was the "perfection of charity." And one of the definitions of charity (synonymous with love) was harmony. The means to the end were the "rules of the order" which embodied acts of kindness, justice, and sharing—all good practices. It was almost a fantasy world, but we were all so docile it worked. After 10 days we were asked to make the big decision—either stay in the Order, or "go back to the world." All 30 of us elected to stay.

The monastery, a Medieval-looking structure sat high on Stockton Hill, on the outskirts of a beautiful, hilly Minnesota river town, Winona. The "profession day" was August 4, the feast of St. Dominic. The sun was shining and the sky was blue, with only a few white clouds. The wind caught the black cappas and hoods covering our white habits as we waited outside the front door of the Church entrance to the monastery. We were all so innocent, ready to profess our allegiance to the Lord Jesus Christ, and carry out His work on this earth. Our reward would be an eternal life of love and happiness—union with God. We were ready.

After the holy sacrifice of the Mass, the brothers, one by one, prostrated themselves at the feet of the Prior to accept this holy vocation and enter into the Dominican Order, a revered institution in the Catholic Church since the early 13th Century.

We were about to enter a solemn ceremony called "the investiture of the habit." In the ceremony we were given the monk's robe, and told that we would have one year to live the religious life and prepare for the vows of poverty, chastity, and obedience. Even though we didn't take the vows at that investiture, we were told about the vows. The very word puts some "fear of the Lord" in you.

The Prior said, "You used to think of your body as flesh and bone. Now you must think of it as a stick or a stone." *Now* I'm amazed I didn't get up from my prone position and run out the door. *Then* I gladly assented to this great calling.

Seminary lasted eight years. We sublimated our bodily desires by immersing ourselves in the teachings of Aristotle and Thomas Aquinas. Sports and cold showers also helped. Celibacy was really not that difficult, since the only women we saw were the sisters of classmates who might come to our monastery for an occasional Sunday visit. And it seemed unseemly to lust after a classmate's sister.

Of course, "wet dreams" (a phrase invented by Catholics) occurred as our source of sexual pleasure, but they were not sinful, since we could not control our bodily functions when we slept.

When we weren't studying, our days were filled with chanting of the divine office in Latin, half-hour periods of meditation, daily mass, and some pretty decent meals.

Before I knew it, the one-year spiritual formation called the *Novitiate*, in Winona, the three years of philosophy in River Forest, Illinois, and the three years of Theology in Dubuque, Iowa were over. We were ready for Ordination to the priesthood in the summer of 1965. I was excited and ready to work. John F. Kennedy, our Catholic secular saint had been assassinated, but Robert Kennedy and Martin Luther King were leading the charge to make the world a better place. Pope John XXIII had opened the doors and windows of the Catholic Church, and our Christianity was relevant and powerful.

My first assignment during my "young dad" year—the year after ordination, but before our fourth and last year of theology, was to a settlement house in Chicago, Illinois. It was right in the middle of the black ghetto on Washington Ave, 35 blocks west of Lake Michigan. Three of us Dominicans joined seven lay volunteers for a service internship at the Martin De Poress House. There we taught kids sports, prayer, and songs. One of my co-workers, Sue Lynch, told us that when she was teaching a class of youngsters about the Holy Eucharist, she said, "Now if you go to Church on Sunday, the priest will say, 'Hoc est enim corpus meum' *this is My body*, and at that point, the bread will turn into the body and blood of Jesus. In other words, the bread turns into God."

A little boy in her class who had not been planning on going to Church on Sunday turned to his friend and said, *"I'm going. This I gotta see!"*

After the last year of theology, in Dubuque, I was even more ready to get out in the world. My assignment that summer brought me to Monet Ferry, Louisiana. I was under the tutelage of a Fr. Albert, an elderly Croatian priest. We had two parishes to service, the one he lived in, and the black parish about 10 miles South of Monet Ferry.

With Martin Luther King, Jr. riding high, and President Lyndon Johnson in the White House, I felt emboldened to preach the new gospel to the new south. But not all my parishioners shared my enthusiasm. When I took the black children to the "whites only" swimming hole, I heard about it from my pastor. When I told the black housekeeper that she should go to communion with the rest of the congregation instead of going *last* and at the side railing, she respectfully bowed her head and said, "No thank you, Father." When preaching integration, I'd notice the "red necks" pacing back and forth in the back of the Church, and they didn't look happy.

I was beginning to see some of the warts on my beloved Catholic Church. Why did they tolerate segregation with a black and a white church? Why was Cardinal Spellman of New York blessing the warships heading toward Vietnam, when my heroes, the Jesuit Berrigan brothers, were condemning the war as unjust? With the excitement of the "aggiornamento" (the updating of the Catholic Church) came some uneasiness that we didn't have all the answers—that even priests could differ on what was moral and not moral.

And the emphasis on obedience, dogma and ritual ran head-on into the issues of service, examination, and questioning. Was the church merely perpetuating its power, or really serving the flock?

• • •

After that invigorating summer, I was given my first permanent assignment as a parish priest. Martin Luther King and Bobby Kennedy enthralled me, so my superiors sent me to a "poverty parish" in Minneapolis, Minnesota—Holy Rosary Church.

I arrived in late August to be met by the pastor, Fr. John Morganthaler. "Morgy" as we all called him, was a gentle soul who had taught me Latin in high school. I was pleased to have him as a pastor. He was a serious man (I'm surprised that he let people call him "Morgy") and didn't have much personality, but his kindness was genuine so people liked him. He greeted me warmly, showed me my 9-foot by 12-foot "cell" with a sink in it, and told me we would discuss my responsibilities at 8:00 the next morning.

Besides my normal duties to say Mass, visit the sick, and perform weddings and funerals, Morgy put me in charge of the Holy Name Society (a group of about 100 men who sponsored Tuesday night bingo games—the revenue from which kept the parish alive), the Third Order of St. Dominic (an association of about 100 women who prayed together at a monthly meeting), and the Youth Club (a collection of about 100 high school students who wanted to dance and keep up grammar-school friendships). I was delighted. The priests at my Chicago parish, *Our Lady Help of Christians*, were always treated with a great deal of respect, and Holy Rosary folks followed suit.

The Youth Club grabbed most of my time. The kids hadn't had a young priest in charge of their club, and they seemed starved for attention. We had a large Church basement with a wonderful stage. Putting on dances became our prime activity. The dances where not only fun, with the latest rock and roll music, but they made a profit to fund our field trips. We'd go to Red Wing, Minnesota to visit the juvenile center there, drive to Stillwater, Minnesota to watch the boats on the St. Croix river, and even took a bus to Chicago one time to visit the youth at the Martin de Poress House in Chicago.

One night we stayed up all night in the Church basement with the youth clubs from St. Peter Claver Church in St. Paul—a black Church run by a good friend, Fr. Ed Flahavan—and a white suburban Church, supervised by a doctor Bob Phelps. Some of the parents of the Holy Rosary teens didn't mind my mixing their kids with the white suburban kids, but they got nervous when I'd mix them with the juvenile delinquents in the Red Wing detention center, or the blacks from another poor parish, St. Peter Claver. The parents wanted their kids to "marry up" the social scale, not "marry down." Mixing these kids of blue-collar families with delinquents or blacks was not their parents' idea of improving their chances in life.

At one meeting of the fathers and sons of our Youth Club, we invited a cub reporter from the Minneapolis Tribune, Dave Mona. He listened to the fathers complain that their sons were smoking, drinking, even skipping school, and to the sons whine that the fathers never took them fishing anymore, and didn't seem to care or understand their needs as teenagers. Toward the end of the meeting one creative boy threw out the challenge that they do something *together*. After some discussion they decided to rent a little storefront on Lake Street and start a drop-in center and dance hall. The reporter was intrigued, and wrote up a full-length story about this exchange—names and all. With all that publicity in print, the boys and their parents were obliged to follow through. Within one month they rented the space and began fixing and painting it up. This called for another story in the Tribune—this time, an even longer one, with three big pictures. The kids were thrilled. To this day, 35 years later, that drop-in center still exists—although we had to change the name from *The Psychotic City* to *The City*. (It was hard to raise money with the word "psychotic" in the name.)

Morgy could tolerate my involvement with *The City*, but he had a harder time with some of my other extracurricular activities. The one that bothered him most was my protesting the war in Vietnam. One night Vice President Hubert Humphrey was coming to the world famous Guthrie Theater to enjoy *MacBeth* (or was it *Hamlet*?). A friend of mine, Jim Luger, asked me if I would come in my roman collar to join his group of demonstrators to greet Humphrey with signs linking the blood in the Shakespeare play to the current bloodletting in Vietnam. I had never been in a demonstration before, but Jim assured me that the demonstrators would all be well-dressed, classy people who would not degrade my reputation. Courage and respectability were the only things needed. "What the heck, I thought, Jesus was a pretty non-violent guy. I think He would go.

I went, and unfortunately, my name got in the paper the next day. That newspaper story, plus the sign in my front window which read, "White Racism Must Go," started Morgy thinking that I (and he) might be better off if I were assigned to a parish down in New Orleans, Louisiana with a pastor named, John "crusher" Connolly. Crusher got his nickname because he used to crush his knuckles into the top of the heads of the kids at my old high school, Fenwick. Crusher would be much more able to sit on this "young Turk" than Morgy would.

When Morgy told me of the plan to send me down South, I told a parishioner, Marie Manthey. Marie said, "Do you want to fight it?"

I replied, "Maybe. What do you have in mind?"

"If we can get enough of your influential friends to call Morgy, or his boss, I'll bet we can get him, or them, to reverse themselves. You have a lot of friends who would call or write letters. I'd be happy to contact them so you can stay out of it. I'd only use as much pressure as necessary, increasing the heat gradually. You know—Saul Alinsky style."

"If you're willing to do it, I'd be happy to watch. I'd really like to stay here," I said with my devilish smile.

I gave Marie a list of names and phone numbers and she went to work, calling a city council member, the head of the NAACP, Dr. Phelps, the head of the Third Order of St. Dominic, The president of the Holy Name Society, and a few other community leaders.

When Morgy was feeling the stress, but wasn't quite ready to reverse himself, Marie talked the Youth Club into setting up tables outside of Church to collect signatures from the parishioners asking Morgy to let me stay. That move was unbearable. Morgy hopped on a plane to Chicago that Sunday to go have a talk with the Provincial. That night I got a call from the Provincial asking me to fly to Chicago and talk over my new assignment. Naturally I had to say "yes," but for some fortunate reason I asked if I could bring my classmate, Fr. Timothy McCarthy, with me to help plead my case. The Provincial granted my wish. I was delighted because Tim, a former captain of Notre Dame's basketball team, was very smart and well respected. Tim was solidly in my corner, and had even written up my story for publication in a weekly liberal Catholic newspaper. It wasn't the *National Catholic Reporter,* but it was a similarly respected journal. Tim must have known the editor, because he had this agreement with the paper that if I got to stay at Holy Rosary, the paper would not run the story. If I had to obey the order to move, then they would print Fr. Tim's account.

The write-up was in their hands. I agreed to call them as soon as the meeting was over and tell them *print* or *no print*. Their deadline for a decision was 5 p.m. Our meeting started at 3:30 p.m. The timetable left no room to maneuver.

When Tim and I entered the room, seated there were Fr. Gilbert Graham, the Provincial (like a bishop to Order priests), Fr. Fandel (assistant Provincial), and a grim-faced Morgy. They outnumbered us 3 to 2, but those were much better odds than if my friend Fr. Tim hadn't been there.

After the normal pleasantries had been exchanged, Morgy stated his case against me. The essence of his case was that I was more interested in the secular issues of civil rights and stopping the war in Vietnam than I was in the sacramental ministry. The argument Tim and I made was that the work with minorities and the saving of lives in Vietnam were priestly work. And, as long as I wasn't neglecting my priestly duties of saying mass, visiting the sick and taking care of the parish programs, there shouldn't be a problem. Fandel seemed like he was on a witch-hunt, but Graham seemed impartial. When he asked Morgy if I was "a good priest" fulfilling my duties, Morgy, honest man that he was, had to admit there was no neglect, and that I was well liked by most of the parishioners. Graham was genuinely perplexed. The traditional wisdom was to support the older authority. Morgy was even older than Graham, and had earned the respect of all. As 4:45 p.m. approached there was a long silence. Morgy's head hung down. Tim and I were focused on Graham. Fandel looked angry. I sensed we were winning.

"I've decided to let you stay," blurted out Graham.

Hallelujah! I thought. What a victory! At that time, within the Church tradition, a victory like that was unheard of. Fr. Tim and I thanked all three of them profusely, shook their hands, and raced down the stairs to the nearest phone so we could call the newspaper.

"Kill the story," I told the editor. "We won. I can stay."

"Congratulations," he said. I could tell there wasn't much joy in his voice. He had just lost a fascinating story.

• • •

One final story is about my last year in the priesthood and at Holy Rosary. During March of 1968, I attended a weekend seminar at the Catholic Youth Center on East 22nd Street and Park Avenue, in south Minneapolis. These seminars were called "love fests," but the common understanding was that this meant "Christian love," or "agape," an altruistic *sharing and caring* love. But when people of both genders come and spend a weekend together, sharing intimate thoughts, there is a risk that other kinds of love (amicitia [friendship] or eros [romantic attraction]) may be awakened. This is what happened between me and a young female volunteer named Phoebe Ann Yaeger. Phoebe was working in Amarillo Texas as an "Extension Volunteer, sometimes called a "lay volunteer" in a Catholic parish. Phoebe preferred to call herself a "lay volunteer" and then watch for the reaction from her listener. Her pastor had sent her up to her home state of Minnesota for the seminar and a bit of "R and R" with her parents in Wabasha, Minnesota. She seemed brash, smart, funny and interested in youth. She said she was spending the summer in Minneapolis and asked if I knew of any job openings. I told her that The City, Inc. might be interested in a temporary executive director. She was interested, and over the spring we made the arrangement for the hire. Long story short, the friendship eventually turned into a romantic relationship and we married shortly after I left the priesthood. If it weren't for the "love fest" at the Catholic Youth Center, you, my boy, would not exist.

• • •

I've already told you (in my letter about "forks in the road") the details of how I left the priesthood in August of 1968. Right now I'd like to say something about the first three transition years, and end by telling you about the biggest job of my career (25 years with Project for Pride in Living), my present job with the One Percent Club, and a few last paragraphs about my personal life.

My very first job after leaving the priesthood was with Honeywell, Inc., a multinational manufacturer of heating controls, among other things. I got to know many of the top executives of large corporations through the Minneapolis Urban Coalition, a group of high-powered individuals and corporations formed after the riots of 1968. Jim Binger and Steve Keating of Honeywell, the Pillsbury brothers, and some of the Dayton brothers were among my acquaintances when they became interested in inner city issues and social unrest. Honeywell had a great reputation for hiring minorities. I thought I'd like to be part of their team.

I got the job on the condition that I'd start working in the factory, and then when an opening in personnel occurred, I would be the first to be considered. I liked the idea. First because I had never experienced a job in a factory (and worker-priests were the rage in France), and secondly, it would give me the feel of what these black recruits would have to face if Honeywell could hire them in big numbers.

The first couple days on the job I was drilling holes, sanding metal, and learning a bit of welding. I had no idea what I was working on. Then I asked the supervisor, "What are these things?"

He said, "These are the so-called 'mother bombs,' the containers that carry the anti-personnel bombs." I was aghast. Here was this committed peace activist actually working on something that would maim and kill people in Vietnam. I immediately called the guy who hired me, a vice-president named Sam Vitale, and asked him if there was an opening in personnel, and told him why I couldn't continue working at that factory. He informed me that no such opening existed, so I gave notice and was out by the end of the week.

After a brief jaunt (six months) as the Twin Cities' community organizer for Cesar Chavez and the grape boycott, my career in altruism hit a speed bump—I actually sold mutual funds for Investors Diversified Services, (IDS). One day, when I was trying to sell to a friend of mine, Jim Luger, he asked, "how do you make your money?" I explained that when a customer put $100 a month into a mutual fund, I got a $10 per month commission for a while. He said, "Why don't we just get 100 of your progressive friends to give you $10 a month—invest in *you* rather than in corporate America?" Their "return on investment" would be in "psychic income" from knowing they had done some good in the world, rather than in dollar income. We wrote to 200 of my friends and 100 of them said yes. I quit my job with IDS and returned to trying to do good rather than well.

With 100 financial supporters behind me, but wanting their donations to be tax-deductible, I formed a small non-profit corporation and called it Advocate Services, Inc. There I had the freedom to do just about anything I wanted to do in the areas of race, peace, and poverty. Jim Luger, the peace activist/manufacturer's representative gave me office space at Nicollet and 25th Street, and I was off and running. I would organize protests through Clergy and Laity Concerned About Vietnam, be an advocate for a minority person if they thought they were discriminated against, or help start another non-profit, like Project for Pride in Living (PPL).

After three years in advocacy and community organizing, I gave a talk at St. Joan of Arc Catholic Church. I preached about the poverty in Minneapolis with the refrain being, "This is not in Calcutta, but in Minneapolis." After Mass, one of the parishioners, Ted Pouliot, came up to me and invited me to his house for dinner. He said he had goods from his home and business that he could donate, and had friends in business who would probably do the same if it were tax-deductible. I took him up on the offer, and within two months the goods were flowing in so fast we had to start another non-profit, and called it "Project for Pride in Living." We quickly focused on work whose mission was *to help low-income people become self-sufficient by addressing their job, housing, and neighborhood needs.*

At first, I was just on the board, of which Ted Pouliot was the first chair. But after our first 18 months of volunteer work, Hal Greenwood, President of Midwest Federal Savings and Loan, decided to strengthen our capacity by giving us a $5,000 grant and a $1 million line of credit, parts of which could be turned into mortgages as we rehabilitated and sold the homes. A million dollars! I had no idea what that could do, but I decided I should release my Advocate Services funders, and switch over to become a paid staff person of PPL. The board agreed, and I had a real job again.

There I took a roller-coaster ride from a yearly budget of $12 thousand to a budget of $12 million twenty-five years later. We grew from a staff of one to 200 employees; from a board of 6 to a board of 46; from a couple of donors and volunteers to several hundred funders and volunteers. There were lots of fights—and hugs—with neighborhood groups, the board of directors, rich funders, poor clients, and friends who were employees. I emerged with lots of battle scars, but feeling pretty good about all of it. At 60, five years after my heart attack, I retired from PPL.

For 30 years I had been working with the poor. Then a friend of mine, Tom Lowe, brought me a book by Claude Rosenberg, Jr. titled *Wealthy and Wise*. After reading it, Tom pointed out that if the top taxpayers in the country donated just one percent of their net worth, annually, it would generate another $100 billion for the non-profits serving our community. Then we started calculating what it might be in Minnesota, and we came up with a figure of close to $1 billion a year. Rosenberg called this concept of net-worth giving, *new tithing*. He argued that high-net-worth people like Bill Gates, Jr., who was worth $100 billion at the time, was probably taking a million dollars a year in income, (and tithing at 10 percent or $100,000), but if he gave from net worth, at just one percent, he'd be giving away $1 billion per year.

Shortly after that I ran the concept past one of Minneapolis' best philanthropists, Kenneth Dayton, and asked him if Rosenberg's concept made sense, and if one percent was a reasonable standard. He answered affirmatively, so I asked a follow-up question. "Would you be willing to sign a commitment to that standard, and go public in the *Star-Tribune* with that commitment? His answer, "If you can get nine of my peers to sign the same commitment, I'll do it."

After he signed the pledge, I was able to bring subsequent signers to a total of 37. We were now ready to go to the *Star-Tribune*. Fortunately, the newspaper has a reporter, Bob Franklin, who is intensely interested in philanthropy. He offered to come to our next meeting and do some interviews and send a photographer out. He and his editors were so impressed that we got a front-page story with three pictures in the Sunday edition of the paper. The first edition even made it the headline story.

After the story broke (in November 1997), we had all kinds of interest. This inspired us to start a "club" of high-net-worth individuals who were willing to give away one percent or more of their net worth annually. Now, after years of being a supplicant, I was suddenly working with the rich. We decided to incorporate, and I became the volunteer executive director. Now, after almost 6 years of growth, by adding 10 members per month since the club's birth, we have grown to more than 700 members. In the years 1999, 2000, and 2001 we brought in an extra $36,000,000 to the community according to our anonymous surveys. Soon we'll be able to claim to have generated an extra $100 million for the community's charities. We're the only such club in the country.

There's one more very important thing I have to say before I end this—something that should come as no surprise: Your mother and I loved you from day one, and continue to do so. Even our friends and relatives have told us, "One thing that child isn't suffering from is lack of love."

And I don't mean that your mother and I should get all the credit for that. You've certainly done your part. You've been a lovable kid. You didn't make all the right choices along the way, but you did your best. You never got into serious trouble. You never embarrassed us. You always lived a balanced life of work, play, and leisure. What more could parents ask for? And, after all, this correspondence is not being reviewed by a corrections official. Maybe I should thank you now. Thank you.

With love,

Dad

AFTERWORD

by Burt Cohen

If you're reading this page, it probably means you have already formed some interesting opinions about my friend Joe Selvaggio. On the other hand, it could also mean you're just one of those people who like to read things starting from the back, in which case you know nothing about Joe and are already beginning to regret your decision to buy this book, even though it was on the close-out table.

In any event, you either have discovered or are about to discover that Joe is a one-of-a-kind character and a man who has devoted his life to helping those in need by extracting money from those who have it. He likes to think of himself as a modern day Robin Hood, taking money from the rich and giving it to the poor, especially to those who use it to leverage their way to a better, more fulfilling life. Unlike Robin Hood, however, he doesn't wear green tights, although he has been seen in some pretty bizarre outfits.

I first met Joe some years ago, when he was running the Project for Pride in Living (PPL)enterprise in Minneapolis. I thought the initials stood for parsnips, potatoes, and legumes, and stopped in for lunch. What I found out was that PPL is a truly remarkable organization devoted to helping disadvantaged people hold their heads up high by enabling them to move into decent housing or be trained for well-paying jobs. The program, which Joe conceptualized, started, ran and nurtured over many years, became a brilliant success, a model for other programs elsewhere, and a source of pride and strength to both the individuals it serves and to all of us in this community. Joe built PPL by believing he could not fail, a philosophy that reinforced in him the determination to always persist and to never give up.

Actually, the only known case of Joe's giving up on anything had to do with the movie deal. He just recently told me, in absolute confidence and with the understanding I would disclose it to no one, that his greatest fantasy (alright, second-greatest fantasy) is to have Warner Bros. film the story of his life, starring that Selvaggio look-alike Tom Cruise. Warners briefly considered the idea, but said the role of Joe would be played by Queen Latifah, which would require a few changes in the story. Joe himself was to play the part of the evil landlord; but the negotiations eventually broke down when Joe refused to do the nude scene because of his dermatitis.

At this point, if you haven't already asked the bookstore clerk for your money back, you'll be fascinated to learn that when Joe finally decided to turn the PPL reins over to someone else, he immediately started yet another innovative concept, The One Percent Club. This is an organization whose sole purpose is to encourage people to give more each year—one percent of their assets, or five percent of their income (whichever is greater)—to not-for-profit causes of their choice. There is no reporting, no dues, no meetings, and only one obligation: to be more generous to charitable causes by giving to a standard. Largely because of Joe's relentless efforts, the organization is strong and growing, and the resulting benefits throughout our community and beyond are enormous.

Joe's commitment to those in need, his humility, his perseverance, and his weird sense of humor all combine to make him a remarkable citizen, albeit one who really knows how to hurt a guy. When he asked me to write this afterword, I told him I'd much prefer to write the foreword. He thought about it for a minute and then said no, the foreword was too important to assign to me. "Hardly anyone reads the afterword," he added, "so I think that's the ideal place for someone of your talent.'

The problem is, he was right.

Burt Cohen is the Founding Publisher of MSP Communications, which publishes *Mpls/St Pau*l Magazine and *Twin Cities Business Monthly.*